Martin Luther King, Jr.

Martin Luther King, Jr.

Amy Pastan

DK PUBLISHING, INC.

LONDON, NEW YORK, MELBOURNE,
MUNICH, AND DELHI

Designed for DK Publishing, Inc.
by Mark Johnson Davies

Series Editor : Beth Sutinis
Editorial Assistant : Madeline Farbman
Art Director : Dirk Kaufman
Publisher : Chuck Lang
Creative Director : Tina Vaughan
Photo Research : Tracy Armstead
Production : Chris Avgherinos
DTP Designer : Milos Orlovic

First American Edition, 2004

13 14 15 14

023-DD180-Aug/2004

Published in the United States
by DK Publishing
345 Hudson St., New York, New York 10014

Library of Congress Cataloging-in-Publication Data
Pastan, Amy.
  DK biography : Martin Luther King, Jr. / written by Amy
Pastan.-- 1st American ed.
   p. cm. -- (DK biography)
  Includes bibliographical references (p.   ) and index.
  ISBN: 978-0-7566-0342-7 (PB) ISBN: 978-0-7566-0491-2 (HC)
  1. King, Martin Luther, Jr., 1929-1968--Juvenile literature. 2.
African Americans--Biography--Juvenile literature. 3. Civil rights
workers--United States--Biography--Juvenile literature. 4.
Baptists--United States--Clergy--Biography--Juvenile literature. 5.
African Americans--Civil rights--History--20th century--Juvenile
literature. I. Title: Martin Luther King, Jr. II. Title. III. Series.
  E185.97.K5P265 2004
  323'.092--dc22
                                           2004007983

Color reproduction by GRB Editrice s.r.l., Italy
Printed and bound in China
by South China Printing Co., Ltd.

Cover photos: Border images from left to right: ©AP Wide World: a;
©Bettmann/Corbis: b; ©AFP/CORBIS: c; ©Bettmann/Corbis: d;
©Raymond Gehman/Corbis: e; ©Bettmann/Corbis: f, g; ©Flip
Schulke/Corbis: h; ©William Lovelace/Hulton Archive/Getty Images: i.
Front jacket, main image: ©Time Life Pictures/Getty Images. Spine:
©Bettmann/Corbis. Back jacket, main image: ©William
Lovelace/Hulton Archive/Getty Images.

Discover more at
www.dk.com

Contents

chapter 1

Being Black in Dixie

As a little boy he could slug a baseball and sing a hymn. He would recite prayers at the dinner table, and then slide down the banister right after supper. Growing up on Auburn Avenue, he played catch with friends in his backyard, walked to his father's church on Sundays, and knew all his neighbors.

But beyond that safe world, young Martin Luther King, Jr., discovered another that would not accept him because his skin was dark. His mother told him that the world would change one day. "I'm going to turn this world upside down," he promised her. Many years later, as leader of America's civil rights movement, he did.

Martin was born in Atlanta, Georgia, in 1929, at a time when segregation laws kept Negroes—the name commonly used for black people at that time—from having the same rights as white people. The segregation laws under which Martin lived were called "Jim Crow," the name of a character in a minstrel show of the early 1800s. In such shows, white actors painted their faces black and imitated Negroes singing and dancing. This reinforced the negative view of Negroes most whites already had.

The Jim Crow laws passed by state governments in the

SEGREGATION

Segregation is the separation of one group of people from another, usually because of race, class, or religion.

South were upheld by a Supreme Court case of 1896 called *Plessy v. Ferguson*. Homer Plessy, a black man, had been arrested in 1892 for riding in the "white" section of a Louisiana train. The Court ruled that separate facilities—schools, restrooms, water fountains—for blacks and whites were legal as long as they were equal, meaning as long as they offered the same services. These laws went into effect many years after the Civil War, but they had their roots in slavery.

Shortly after North America was settled by Europeans, Africans were kidnapped by slave traders and sold to whites who forced them to work without pay. For about 250 years—from the 1600s to the end of the Civil War—slave owners claimed superiority over those in bondage. They spread the idea that black people were an inferior, uncivilized race, and they

Jim Crow laws affected nearly all businesses in the South after the Civil War, as the "colored only" sign on this shack shows.

used brute force to keep blacks from gaining their freedom. Slavery died out in the North by the nineteenth century, but southerners were dependent on slave labor to run their large farms, or plantations. The Union victory in the Civil War was supposed to have opened the door to greater freedom for black people, but the South was not eager to change and adopted the Jim Crow segregation laws. In *Plessy v. Ferguson*, blacks protested that the laws were not "equal," just "separate," but it took years—and many more court cases—before their outcries were heard.

Black people had held high hopes for the future back in 1863, when President Abraham Lincoln signed the Emancipation Proclamation, granting freedom to southern slaves. The North

As a candidate for the U.S. Senate in 1858, Abraham Lincoln predicted that the issue of slavery would divide the nation.

was gaining ground in the Civil War and Lincoln's act gave some slaves the courage to leave the plantations. Many of them fought as Union soldiers in the Civil War. Shortly after the Union victory, several constitutional amendments were adopted, granting former slaves the basic rights of United States citizens. The Thirteenth Amendment outlawed slavery; the Fourteenth Amendment protected the rights of newly freed slaves; and the Fifteenth Amendment gave black men the right to vote. Soon black people in the South were running for political

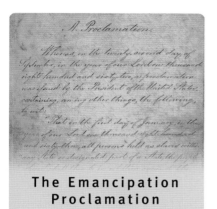

The Emancipation Proclamation

President Lincoln issued the Emancipation Proclamation on January 1, 1863. It declared that all slaves living in Confederate territory "in rebellion against the United States" would be free. Few slave owners acted on the order. The Proclamation was important for what it suggested—that slavery was a central issue of the Civil War, and that slavery was wrong.

office. Fourteen blacks served in the U.S. Congress between 1870 and 1876.

However, the promise of equal citizenship was soon broken. Whites in the southern states were never truly willing to share political power and social circles with blacks. Some politicians worked to keep blacks from getting into office. Violence was used to intimidate poor black people. White supremacist societies were established, such as the Ku Klux Klan (KKK), which was formed by a group of Confederate Army veterans. In the last two decades of the nineteenth century, almost 2,000 blacks were lynched—murdered by mobs—many in front of cheering white spectators. The government did little to stop such crimes.

Some blacks tried to answer such threats with protests and political tactics. W.E.B. DuBois, an African-American scholar who had studied

RACISM

Racism is the belief that one race is superior to another.

at Harvard, was a critic of racism and helped establish the National Association for the Advancement of Colored People (NAACP) in 1910. This organization grew quickly. By the time Martin Luther King, Jr., was in elementary school, there were tens of thousands of members throughout the country. One member was Martin's dynamic father, the Reverend Martin Luther King, Sr. "Mike"

The Kings' house at 501 Auburn Avenue in Atlanta, Georgia. Like many children of his era, Martin Luther King, Jr., was born at home.

King, the respected pastor of the Ebenezer Baptist Church, was involved in local activities to improve conditions for Negroes in Atlanta. He once led several hundred blacks on a voter registration march. He also waged a campaign to raise the salaries of Negro schoolteachers so that their pay would be the same as white teachers'. Young Martin marveled at his father's ability to take a stand on racial issues without angering whites in the community.

For Martin, or "M.L." as he was called throughout his childhood, reminders of his place in life were everywhere. To most white people, Negroes didn't have names. They were "boy" or "girl" or, even worse, "nigger." In his neighborhood, M.L. was the son of an esteemed preacher, but downtown he could not even sit at a lunch counter. There were WHITE and

COLORED signs over drinking fountains, on restroom doors, on buses. The colored restrooms weren't cleaned, and the colored sections on buses were in the very back. Movie theaters had colored sections, too, and many barber shops, hotels, and swimming pools were strictly "Whites Only." M.L. discovered that his Victorian-style house on Auburn Avenue was in a section whites referred to as "Nigger Town." In downtown Atlanta, Confederate flags from Civil War times still hung from public buildings, and "Dixie" was played at parades and festivals. Books and movies, such as the award-winning *Gone with the Wind*, glorified the days of Southern plantations and presented a happy picture of slave life.

Although M.L. had loving parents who provided a secure life for their children, there was no escaping the cruelties of Jim Crow. Such unfairness was deeply felt by the sensitive boy. But Reverend King taught his son to stand up for himself.

Under Jim Crow laws, black people were required to use separate facilities, such as water fountains. A person caught violating the laws could lose his job or even be lynched.

FOR COLORED ONLY

Because the law forced him to sit at the back of the bus, "Daddy King" drove his own car instead. When a white police officer stopped Reverend King and demanded, "Boy, show me your license," M.L.'s father pointed to his son and said, "That's a *boy* there. I'm a *man*."

The Kings also taught their children that hate was not an answer to what they called "the race problem." They were deeply religious, and they believed that it was their Christian duty to love all people, even whites. As a child, Martin could not understand this. He knew better than to talk back when white people called him "nigger" or to refuse when they told him to move to the back of the bus, but a fury toward whites was growing inside him.

M.L.'s mother, Alberta Williams King, tried to help her children—Christine, Martin, and Alfred Daniel, called "A.D."—get along in the world of Jim Crow, while making it clear that she disagreed with such laws. The daughter of well-known Atlanta minister A.D. Williams, she was a quiet woman who had received an excellent education. M.L.'s father was a sharecropper's son who left home as a teenager and worked as a laborer. With little education, he

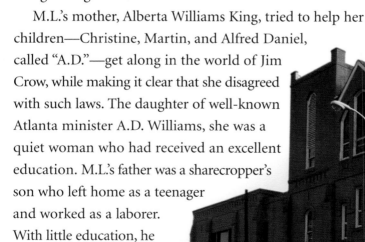

Ebenezer Baptist Church was a site of civil rights activity as early as the late 1800s, when the Reverend A.D. Williams was pastor.

became a self-trained preacher, talked his way into college, and then courted Alberta. They were married in 1926 at A.D. Williams's church, Ebenezer Baptist. The Kings moved in with Alberta's parents at 501 Auburn Avenue. There, Christine was born in 1927, Martin— originally named Michael, like his father— on January 15, 1929, and A.D. in 1930. Mike King, who, in 1934, changed his name to Martin Luther, after the founder of the Protestant religion, wanted his son's name to match. At age five, young Michael officially became Martin Luther King, Jr.

It was also at age five that M.L. formally joined the church. When a guest minister asked the children in Sunday school if they wanted to find salvation, Christine's hand shot up. Not to be outdone by his older sister, M.L. was next to volunteer. Years later, he admitted that his baptism was the result of sibling competition, not religious belief. He also insisted on following Christine to first grade, even though he was too young to be there. He was sent home when his true age was discovered. All three King children adored their grandmother, whom they called "Mama," but M.L. had a special relationship with her. Once, he showed his deep feeling for her when A.D. slid down the banister and accidentally hit Mama, knocking her out cold. M.L., believing his grandma dead, ran upstairs and threw himself out a window.

Fortunately, both boy and grandmother survived, but the family was worried by M.L.'s extreme concern for Mama. M.L. was in seventh grade at the Atlanta University Laboratory School when Mrs. Williams suddenly died of a heart attack. His parents told their grieving son about immortality, assuring him that his grandmother lived in heaven. As an adult, Martin Luther King, Jr., would say that Mama's death had a big impact on his religious beliefs.

King would look back on his childhood as a happy one, but some experiences left their mark. Martin was born just before the stock market crash of 1929 plunged the country into a time of poverty known as the Great Depression. The sight of jobless Negroes on breadlines made him worry about the fate of the poor. Also, in his early years he had a white playmate whose father owned a store near the Kings' house. As the two got older, they entered separate schools. M.L. didn't question this, but when the boy announced that they could no longer be friends, M.L. was devastated. Mike and Alberta tried to explain to their son the complicated rules of race.

After M.L.'s grandmother's death, the Kings moved into a bigger house in a nicer area of Atlanta. M.L. did so well in school that he entered Booker T. Washington High School at age 13. The United States had entered World War II, and many black soldiers were sent overseas to serve in segregated units. On the home front, President Franklin Roosevelt signed an order that prevented racial discrimination in the defense industry. Blacks were making a contribution to the war effort. While M.L's voice deepened and he discovered girls, the country was changing, too. But not fast enough. In eleventh grade, on his way home from winning a speaking contest in Dublin, Georgia, where his topic was "The Negro and the Constitution," M.L. and his teacher were told to give up their bus seats to white riders. M.L. was outraged, but his teacher convinced him to obey the driver's orders. They stood for the entire 90-mile trip back to Atlanta. Later, King said, "That night will never leave my memory."

In 1944, men carry a coffin symbolizing the death of Jim Crow as part of a protest. People had been fighting segregation since the 1800s.

15

chapter 2

Finding Faith

While the war in Europe raged on and more and more young men left their homes for the front, M.L. continued his high school studies. He remained a serious teenager, but discovered that his handsome looks, rich voice, elegant writing style, and stylish tweed suits were powerful magnets for high school girls. He was so vain that his friends nicknamed him "Tweed." This lover of dating and dancing was not thinking about becoming a Baptist preacher, like his stern father. He thought he might make a better doctor or lawyer. It was with these ideas that he entered Morehouse College in Atlanta, the third member of his family—his father and maternal grandfather had gone there—to do so. He was only 15.

Young M.L. had little interest in becoming a preacher like his father until he entered college.

To help pay for his education, Tweed spent the summer before college working on a tobacco farm in Simsbury, Connecticut. It was his first time away from home. There were no Jim Crow laws in the North. M.L. was delighted to discover that he could go into the city on the weekends and eat at a high-class restaurant, just like white people.

He wrote to his father: "On our way here we saw some things I had never anticipated to see. After we passed Washington there was no discrimination at all. The white people here are very nice. We go to any place we want to and sit anywhere we want to."

Although young King may have been glad at the end of the summer to give up working in the hot tobacco fields, he was depressed during the trip home to Atlanta. On the train from New York going South, he could ride wherever he pleased, but when the train came to Washington, D.C., he had to change to a Jim Crow car. When he asked to be served in the dining car, he was seated behind a curtain. That curtain was like a slap in the face. He began to see that he could not accept segregation because the colored waiting rooms, dining cars, and rest rooms were not just separate from those used by white people; they were not equal. Being separated because of his skin color was an attack on his dignity and self-respect.

Morehouse College was having a crisis the September that King entered the freshman class. With so many young men serving in the military overseas, enrollment was low, and the school needed to fill classes in order to pay expenses. For this reason, King was admitted to Morehouse directly from his junior year of high school. He was an eager and intelligent young man, but he was shocked to learn that his reading skills—acquired at colored-only schools—were only at the eighth-grade level.

Morehouse opened King's eyes. While Jim Crow was always a force to be reckoned with in the South, the Morehouse campus gave King a sense of freedom. There, race was openly discussed, and the injustices of segregation were freely voiced. For his first two years in college, King wrestled with career choices. His work on the Intercollegiate Council, a group that worked to achieve racial justice, brought him into contact with white people who truly supported this effort. His long-time anger toward whites began to dissolve and he saw that cooperation among races might be possible. He felt that he could play a major role in bridging barriers between the races.

Benjamin Mays, president of Morehouse, and George Kelsey, King's philosophy professor, were both ministers,

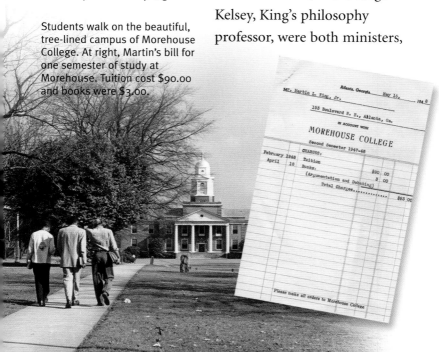

Students walk on the beautiful, tree-lined campus of Morehouse College. At right, Martin's bill for one semester of study at Morehouse. Tuition cost $90.00 and books were $3.00.

and both had a huge effect on their passionate pupil, who wanted to serve society. Under their influence, King decided to enter the ministry. He knew that Negro preachers were often the voice of the community and formed a powerful network for southern blacks. Daddy King was overjoyed by this news and called his son to the pulpit to preach a trial sermon. King was already a powerful speaker. His audition was a huge success. He was ordained at age 18 and made assistant pastor of Ebenezer.

King graduated from Morehouse in 1948, the same year Harry Truman became the first American president to speak at an NAACP convention. It was also in 1948 that the term "civil rights" was first used to describe the struggle of blacks for equality in society. The fact that the president was paying attention to race issues boosted the spirits of southern Negroes who hoped that the post-World War II years would bring greater freedoms. King entered Crozer Theological Seminary in Chester, Pennsylvania, at age 19. He felt that additional education was necessary in order to succeed in the ministry, but he also wanted to attend a school for whites to prove that he was as good as anyone— of any color.

It was at Crozer that King discovered the teachings of

Mohandas K. Gandhi

As a young man, Mohandas K. Gandhi (1869–1948) suffered discrimination that drove him to fight injustice. He rallied the people of India to use his philosophy of *ahisma*—nonviolence—as a weapon against the rule of the British Empire. Gandhi became a spiritual leader to the poor, who called him Mahatma, or "great soul."

Mohandas K. Gandhi, whose philosophy of nonviolent resistance had brought about great social change in India. Gandhi led many successful campaigns against the oppressive British government in India, winning rights for Indians by refusing to cooperate with injustice. By freeing oneself of hatred of one's opponents, Gandhi said, one could work for the good of all mankind.

King was impressed by Gandhi's ideas and began to see that he could adopt these principles in his own life. Using Gandhi's methods, he could take Jesus' message of "love your enemy" to a new level.

King graduated at the top of his class at Crozer in 1951 and won a scholarship to continue his studies. He decided to pursue a doctoral degree at Boston University. Boston, a great northern city that was a center of the antislavery

movement before the Civil War, did not have Jim Crow laws. Yet blacks there still experienced racial discrimination.

In later years, King recalled the difficulty of finding a place to live in the city. When a landlord discovered that a Negro was interested in renting his property, suddenly it was no longer available. But King did not get involved in racial politics during that period. He was concerned with his career—and with finding an appropriate wife.

Coretta Scott was not Martin's first serious girlfriend, but she had all the qualities that mattered to him in choosing a wife—"character, intelligence, personality, and beauty." A student at the highly regarded New England Conservatory of Music, she was studying to become a classical singer. Coretta grew up on a farm in Alabama. Her father had worked hard to send her away from the cotton fields to Antioch College in Ohio. Hoping that Martin would end up with a girl from one of the better black families in Atlanta, Daddy King fought the relationship. But Martin put his foot down. When the Kings realized the depth of his feeling, they gave in.

Coretta and Martin's wedding was at the Scott family farm near Marion, Alabama. The farm was far from town, and as a child, Coretta had to walk five miles each day to attend school.

Coretta and Martin were married at the Scotts' home in Alabama on June 18, 1953. Because there were no honeymoon suites available for Negroes in the South, they spent their wedding night at a friend's funeral parlor.

Coretta had only one more year until graduation, and Martin was finishing his doctoral work. That last year in Boston, King found himself torn between the directions his future should take. He'd been offered teaching posts as well as positions as a preacher. One of the stronger job offers came from the Dexter Avenue Baptist Church in Montgomery, Alabama. The Dexter Avenue church appealed to Martin because it had a long history in the southern black community. Many famous ministers had served there.

Located in the heart of the former Confederacy, just across the street from the Alabama State Capitol, the brick building was erected during Reconstruction, the era just after the Civil War. For Martin and Coretta, both southerners, there was only one drawback to accepting the pastorate at Dexter—it would mean moving back to the world of Jim Crow.

Why would King return to live under conditions that he had found intolerable since childhood? He asked himself that question, and Coretta did the same. In the end, they felt that the South was their home. They could either turn their backs on the problems there, or they could use their education and experience to solve those problems.

Besides, they felt that the climate was changing in the South, and if change came, they wanted to be a part of it.

The reality of living in Montgomery, however, was discouraging to the Kings. Seeing black people at the back of the bus made their hearts sink. King was upset by his congregation's lack of involvement in the community. He became an active member in the local NAACP and urged his church members to do the same. He insisted that every member of Dexter become a registered voter, at a time when many blacks did not vote. With enormous energy, he created committees and clubs to foster community spirit and raise money for church and educational programs. The parishioners were in awe—their young preacher had given the church new life in a matter of weeks, and his electrifying sermons held them spellbound.

King had preached his first sermon as Dexter's pastor in May 1954. That same month the United States Supreme Court handed down

Construction on Dexter Avenue Baptist Church began in 1883. Church members helped by hauling bricks discarded by city workers who were repaving Dexter Avenue.

its ruling in *Brown v. Board of Education* of Topeka, Kansas, which outlawed segregation in public schools.

The Court found that "separate" educational facilities are not necessarily "equal" and that separating black children "solely because of their race generates a feeling of inferiority as to their status in the community that may affect their hearts and minds in a way very unlikely ever to be undone."

With this language, the famous *Plessy v. Ferguson* ruling of 1896 was, in effect, reversed. It was a major attack on Jim Crow, and a major victory for the country's Negroes.

There was little time for celebration. Although King called the Court's ruling "a noble and sublime decision," angry white southerners rejected it. Most whites did not want their children attending schools with black children.

In Mississippi, a White Citizens Council was formed to fight integration, and in other states the Ku Klux Klan burned crosses and attacked innocent Negroes. The State of Alabama joined the pack. Its legislature voted to oppose the Court's decision and keep education segregated at all costs.

A year later, in this tense climate, a 14-year-old Negro was brutally murdered by white men. His crime, so they said, was whistling at a white woman.

Emmett Till, a native of Chicago, had taken the train to Mississippi that summer to visit his relatives. He had no understanding of Jim Crow. When a group of boys dared him to speak to a white woman, he rose to the challenge. Within hours, word was out. Till was dragged from his family's shack. His body was found later in the Tallahatchie River.

Emmett Till in a photograph taken shortly before he was killed on August 28, 1955.

Despite testimony against the white men accused of Till's murder, they were acquitted by an all-white jury. Till became a martyr in what was to become known as the civil rights movement.

The young Reverend King did not yet know that he would have a critical role in this movement. He was rapidly rising to prominence in the Montgomery Negro community and anxiously awaiting the birth of his first child. Yolanda Denise King came into the world on November 17, 1955. Her proud parents called her Yoki.

LYNCHING

A lynching is a killing, often by hanging, at the hands of a mob.

chapter **3**

Mobilizing Montgomery

I t seemed like an ordinary day in Montgomery. Rosa Parks, a Negro seamstress who worked in a downtown depart- ment store, went shopping after work on December 1, 1955. Then she boarded the bus to go home. Mrs. Parks took a seat in the back, just behind the white section. At the next stop,

white riders got on. There were no more seats available in the white section. When the driver told Mrs. Parks to give up her seat, the proper 42-year-old woman and well-respected member of the Negro community simply said, "No." She did not want to stand all the way home, and, more important, she had had enough of Jim Crow.

Mrs. Parks, whose refusal became historic, was arrested and charged with violating the city's segregation laws. E.D. Nixon, a former state

R o s a P a r k s

Born in Tuskegee, Alabama, in 1913, Rosa Parks attended Alabama Teachers College and settled in Montgomery with her husband, Raymond. There she quietly worked for the local NAACP. Mrs. Parks said she had no fear about violating the law on December 1, 1955, because she had already lived with the daily fear of being a black person in the segregated South.

president of the NAACP in Alabama, paid Mrs. Parks's bail and then called the young preacher Martin Luther King, Jr. Nixon was ecstatic. He believed that Mrs. Parks's case could be used to challenge the segregation laws and eventually have them declared unconstitutional by the Supreme Court. A few Negroes had been arrested in the past for refusing to give up their seats, but most had only been charged with "disorderly conduct," which made it impossible to challenge segregation directly. In addition, Nixon told Reverend King, "We have took this type of thing too long already," and he suggested, "The time has come to boycott the buses. Only through a boycott can we make it clear to the white folks that we will not accept this type of treatment any longer." Things were changing in Montgomery.

The day after Rosa Parks's arrest, more than 40 leaders of the Negro community, including King and his best friend, the Reverend Ralph Abernathy, decided to act. They proceeded with a plan to keep black riders off Montgomery's buses. Soon thousands of leaflets were distributed throughout the Negro community: "Don't ride the bus to work, to town, to school, or any place Monday,

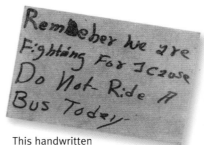

This handwritten sign reminded the black community of Montgomery: "we are fighting for a cause."

December 5." Martin had doubts about the boycott. While he walked the floor with two-week-old Yoki, he worried—could it hurt rather than help the Negro community? Finally, he convinced himself that withdrawing cooperation from an evil system, one that deprived citizens of basic freedoms, was the right thing to do. But would it work?

On Monday, December 5, the Kings got up at dawn. The first bus usually passed their house at 6:00 AM. Martin was getting his coffee in the kitchen when Coretta cried, "Martin, Martin, come quickly!" He ran to the living room. It was unbelievable. The South Jackson bus, usually the most crowded early in the morning, was empty. Fifteen minutes later another bus came along. That one, too, was empty.

Rosa Parks refused to move to the back of this bus, which is now on display at the Henry Ford Museum in Dearborn, Michigan.

A joyous Martin jumped in his car and cruised around the city. There were

GRASSROOTS MOVEMENT

A grassroots movement is an organized effort to accomplish a goal at a local, rather than national, level.

no Negro passengers on any bus line. Instead, the sidewalks were filled with workers walking, thumbing rides—one man was even riding a mule to work. The boycott was a success.

Montgomery's Negro leaders suddenly found themselves in charge of an enormous grassroots movement. With the support of the community so squarely behind them, they had to get organized. They decided to form the Montgomery Improvement Association (MIA), which would direct the boycott. They also voted on a president. Martin Luther King, Jr., the impressive young minister and newcomer to Montgomery, was elected to lead. He had no time to think about how he would shoulder this responsibility. He was to address a mass meeting about the boycott at Holt Street Baptist Church that evening.

Martin agonized over his speech, which he realized was the most important of his career. He wanted to praise the black community for its courage and urge people to continue the boycott. But in keeping with his Christian faith and belief in nonviolence, he needed to stress the importance of protesting without hate. Fifteen thousand people attended the Holt Street meeting that evening. Martin did not disappoint them. He told them that "If we are wrong, the Supreme Court of the nation is wrong. If we are wrong, the Constitution of the United States is wrong. If we are wrong,

God Almighty is wrong," and then reminded them: "As we prepare ourselves for what lies ahead, let us go out with a grim and bold determination that we are going to stick together...." King predicted the boycott would be written up in history books because they—black people from Montgomery—had the "moral courage" to stand up for their rights. The applause was deafening.

King called the bus boycott the "miracle of Montgomery." He was awed by the sight of elderly people hobbling to work rather than break the boycott. One such lady explained, "I'm not walking for myself. I'm walking for my children and grandchildren." This was a new side of black life in Montgomery—one with pride.

When the city prohibited taxis from charging boycotters cheap fares, car pools were formed: Boycott supporters who owned cars picked up passengers at designated places and gave them rides. And some white ladies who couldn't live without their Negro maids aided the boycott by giving their employees a ride to work. Meanwhile, King and the MIA members tried to get the city to change the unfair seating practices on buses. It was an uphill battle.

As months went by, city officials lost patience with the boycott. Once they saw that the protesters would not give up easily, they resorted to harsh tactics. They spread lies about King, saying that he was spending MIA's money on himself. They invented rumors about various Negro preachers, trying to create fighting among MIA's leaders. King was arrested for a minor traffic

violation and experienced the humiliation of being held in a filthy jail cell. There were hate letters from the KKK, threatening phone calls, and finally, on January 30, King's house was bombed. He rushed home from a meeting to find Coretta and Yoki shaken but unharmed. Daddy King said enough was enough and pleaded with Martin to return to the safety of Atlanta, but Martin resolved to stay in Montgomery. He had become the spokesperson for the movement, and he would not leave his people.

In February, the Montgomery County Grand Jury declared the boycott illegal. All participants in the boycott would now face arrest. Of course, King's name was at the top of the list. But the black community had a plan. Negroes began showing up at the jail and turning themselves in. People were proud to be jailed in the cause for freedom. King was convicted of violating the antiboycott law and paid a $500 fine. Television and news cameras recorded him leaving the courtroom with joyous supporters around him singing "We ain't gonna ride the buses no more." Montgomery—and Martin— were making headlines.

His sudden fame as boycott leader was both a

On February 4, 1956, five days after his home had been bombed, King stood on his porch and urged a crowd of supporters to remain calm.

boost and a burden for Martin. In 1955, television had only been in homes for a few years. Suddenly people were able to view events occurring around the world. Seeing King on TV for the first time, Negroes were stunned by his intelligence and inspiring voice. Whites, too, were drawn to him.

King was pleased that Montgomery had drawn the nation's attention—but he wished he had more time to spend with Coretta and Yoki. And fame did not protect him from racists, who flooded his mailbox with hateful letters and threats. Despite such difficulties, King traveled throughout the United States, giving speeches about the Montgomery boycott and the new Negro movement.

By October the boycott was in trouble. There had been a small victory in June, when the Montgomery bus company dropped its segregated seating policy. But an Alabama state court stepped in and said that segregation must continue.

A federal court overruled that decision, but then the city of Montgomery sent an appeal to the Supreme Court. This is just what E.D. Nixon had hoped for back in December

Yoki and Coretta were often on their own due to Martin's busy schedule. After the bombing, Coretta was on constant alert at their house and when out in public.

when Mrs. Parks was arrested. The Fourteenth Amendment was being tested in the highest court of the land. While these legal battles continued, the city came up with ammunition against the car pool. The city claimed that the car pool was a private business and was operating without a license. The city threatened to fine MIA $15,000 for this violation and shut the car pool down. King despaired. With cool fall days and winter on its way, the end of the car pool would mean the end of the boycott. People would return to the buses rather than walk for miles in the cold to get to work.

King was in court fighting to keep the car pool when a reporter rushed in with news from Washington, D.C. He handed Martin a paper announcing the U.S. Supreme Court decision. The justices had declared Alabama's state and local laws regarding segregation on buses unconstitutional. Although King lost the fight for the car pool that day, it no longer mattered. The bigger fight was won. Negroes could ride the buses again—and they could sit wherever they pleased. In the midst of the joyous celebration, King reminded his followers that theirs was not a victory over whites, but "a victory for justice and democracy."

The Supreme Court order angered segregationists. In Montgomery, Ku Klux Klan members put on their robes and hoods and took to the streets of the city. Negroes stood outside their homes and watched the hostile parade, but they did not hide in fear. On December 21, 1956, when the Supreme Court order took effect, Martin Luther King, Jr.,

E.D. Nixon, and the Reverend Ralph Abernathy boarded a city bus and sat up front in what used to be the WHITES ONLY section. Despite a few nasty comments, Negro riders experienced few problems. Amazingly, the buses had been integrated without bloodshed.

Martin and Ralph (right) ride an integrated bus following the Supreme Court order that made segregation of Alabama buses illegal.

The calm did not last long. In the next few weeks terror would strike Montgomery. Klan crosses were seen burning in the night, and several whites picked up guns and fired on city buses. On January 10, Ralph Abernathy was at the Kings' home when he learned that his house and church had been bombed. Four other Negro churches were blown up as well. Bus protests like the one in Montgomery were starting in Birmingham,

The first SCLC headquarters on Auburn Avenue in Atlanta, Georgia. One of the SCLC's main goals was to organize the activities of civil rights groups across the country.

Alabama, and Tallahassee, Florida. It was becoming clear that Negroes needed a strong national organization to unite and represent them.

While bombs continued to shatter the lives of black people in Montgomery, King and his colleagues called together Negro ministers from the southern states. They formed a church-based organization that would raise funds for and give spiritual guidance to a nonviolent movement for racial integration.

Martin's appearance on the cover of *Time* brought national attention to his cause.

It became known as the Southern Christian Leadership Conference (SCLC), and King served as chairman. Now everywhere Martin went, people recognized him, and *Time* magazine featured him on the cover in February 1957. In May, he traveled to Washington. In his first nationwide address, delivered to thousands at the Lincoln Memorial, he pleaded to Congress, "Give us the ballot and we will transform the salient misdeeds of bloodthirsty mobs into the calculated good deeds of ordinary citizens."

Following in Gandhi's Footsteps

Fifteen-year-old Elizabeth Eckford clutched her notebook as she walked toward school on September 4, 1957. It was her first day at Central High in Little Rock, Arkansas. Like most new students, Elizabeth was nervous. But nothing could have prepared the black teenager for the angry white mob that blocked her path to the building. They shouted insults and spat at her. She and eight other black teenagers never made it to the first day of classes.

Disobeying the Supreme Court's *Brown v. Board of Education* ruling, which

A crowd gathers to watch the Little Rock Nine enter Central High School. A legal battle did not stop the nine students from desegregating the school.

declared school segregation illegal, Arkansas Governor Orval Faubus sent in state troops to barricade the school. He vowed to keep the black students out.

A federal judge insisted that Faubus obey the law. The governor withdrew the troops, but did nothing to protect the nine Negro students from the crowd. On the second day of school, the students entered the building, but were soon sent home because the mob outside grew so violent. President Dwight D. Eisenhower realized that the situation was serious.

The Little Rock Nine

The first black students at Central High—Melba Patillo, Elizabeth Eckford, Ernest Green, Gloria Ray, Carlotta Walls, Terrence Roberts, Jefferson Thomas, Minnijean Brown, and Thelma Mothershed—were chosen by the school board from 117 candidates. The decision was based on the students' grades, as well as on their ability to put up with the taunts of their white classmates.

He sent in members of the 101st Airborne Division of the U.S. Army to protect the children. Soldiers accompanied the nine black teenagers to class for the entire school year.

For Martin Luther King, Jr., the incident at Little Rock proved that there was a lot to be done to achieve racial justice in the South. It convinced him that until blacks had political power—until they registered and actually voted—

they would always be held back by people like Governor Faubus. A large Negro votership would ensure that segregationists were not reelected. King and SCLC decided to launch a Crusade for Citizenship, which would educate Negroes about voting and show the country the obstacles Negroes experienced when going to the polls. He knew the crusade would be difficult, but Martin's spirits were high.

Martin had every reason to feel encouraged about the black man's struggle for civil rights, both in the United States and around the world. He had visited the African country of Ghana earlier that year and helped the black nation celebrate its freedom from British rule. He was doubly happy when, on October 23, 1957, Coretta gave birth to their second child, a son they proudly named Martin Luther King III.

Unfortunately, "Little Marty" did not get to spend much time with his father. King was busy working on a book about the bus boycott called *Stride Toward Freedom: The Montgomery Story.*

Martin Luther King, Jr., rests at Harlem Hospital after being stabbed in the chest. He is comforted by his wife Coretta while Ralph Abernathy looks on.

On September 20, 1958, he was signing books at Blumstein's department store in New York, when a Negro woman asked, "Are you Martin Luther King?"

"Yes," he said, and instantly felt a searing pain. The woman had plunged a seven-inch letter opener into his chest. Martin was rushed away in an ambulance. At Harlem Hospital, surgeons removed part of his rib and breastbone to take out the knife, which was so close to his aorta—the heart's main artery—that he would have bled to death if he had so much as moved. Martin received many get well-cards, but there was one he treasured above all:

> Dear Dr. King:
> I am a ninth grade student at White Plains High School. While it shouldn't matter, I would like to mention that I'm a white girl. I read in the paper of your misfortune and of your suffering. And I read that if you had sneezed you would have died. I'm simply writing to say that I'm so happy that you didn't sneeze.

It was later discovered that King's would-be assassin was a mentally ill woman with a sad history. He did not press legal charges against her.

Martin's recovery provided the perfect excuse for a long-awaited trip to India, where he could follow in Gandhi's footsteps. In the countryside, he and Coretta witnessed masses of poor people sleeping on the ground. He learned that they were called untouchables because the higher castes

Untouchables

Hindu religious law separates people by wealth and occupation. One's caste is determined by birth. People born to a low caste cannot join a higher one. Untouchables are considered to have no caste. Despite Gandhi's efforts, many untouchables still live in slums with no clean water, shelter, or health care.

would not have anything to do with them. Gandhi had fought for better treatment of the untouchables. He had refused to eat until leaders of the upper classes agreed to abandon the caste system, which kept these poor Indians at the lowest level of society. Gandhi was close to death from starvation when the Brahmins—members of the highest caste—consented to his terms. Martin thought that the struggles of the American Negro were similar to those of the untouchables, and left India even more determined to use Gandhi's nonviolent methods to help his own people.

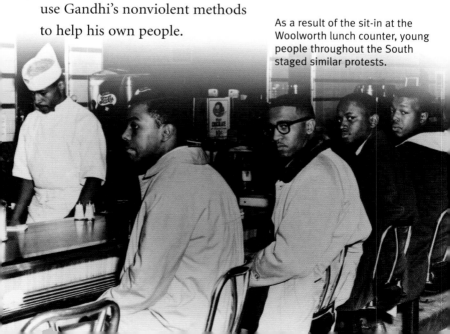

As a result of the sit-in at the Woolworth lunch counter, young people throughout the South staged similar protests.

By 1960 Martin found that he had to make a difficult decision. His duties as leader of the Southern Christian Leadership Conference often took him away from Montgomery and from the congregation of Dexter Avenue Baptist Church. He said good-bye

The first sit-in happened at this Woolworth lunch counter, now on display at the Smithsonian's National Museum of American History.

to Montgomery and returned home to Atlanta, to be close to SCLC headquarters and serve as copastor of Daddy King's church. The family rented a house down the street from Ebenezer Baptist. They were just getting comfortable when news came of a Negro disturbance in North Carolina.

On February 2, 1960, Ezell Blair, Franklin McCain, Joseph McNeil, and David Richmond walked into a Woolworth store in Greensboro, North Carolina, and bought school supplies. They then sat down at the lunch counter and ordered coffee. The four black men, all freshmen at North Carolina A&T College, were told, "We don't serve colored here." The men patiently sat at the lunch counter until the store closed for the evening.

SIT-IN

A sit-in is an organized protest in which people occupy a space or establishment and refuse to leave.

The next day, they returned with 19 other black students. There was still no coffee. By the end of the week, hundreds of black students, as well as several white students, sat in protest at the Woolworth lunch counter. These sit-ins were publicized in radio and television news reports. Inspired by the calm courage of their peers, youth in more than 100 southern cities conducted similar protests in restaurants, parks, swimming pools, and theaters.

Sometimes the students fought to endure the boredom of the long sit-ins, but other times they fought to maintain their composure while whites splattered them with food, burned them with cigarettes, and spat on them. Many looked to a young theology student named James Lawson for guidance. Like Martin Luther King, Jr., Lawson believed in Gandhi's philosophy of nonviolence. He taught students techniques for peacefully putting up with the insults hurled at them and had

A volunteer from the Congress of Racial Equality (CORE) talks to a prospective voter in Baton Rouge, Louisiana, in 1960.

them practice taking special positions that would protect their heads and bodies if they were beaten by club-wielding crowds. The students formed their own organization, the Student Nonviolent Coordinating Committee (SNCC), which had more than 70,000 people participating in sit-ins across the South.

Student leaders from SNCC were planning protests in King's hometown and looked to the SCLC leader for support. This put Martin in a difficult position. He was proud of the students for standing up for their self-respect and their civil rights. But some of the older-generation Negroes—men like Daddy King—were worried that the students' actions would simply anger whites and make it more difficult to fight segregation in schools and at the polls.

On October 19, 1960, King made up his mind. He walked into Rich's department store in downtown Atlanta and sat at the WHITES ONLY lunch counter. He and 75 students were promptly hauled off to jail and charged with trespassing. A few days later, the prisoners were told that the mayor was willing to work out a deal with downtown merchants to desegregate the lunch counters. Feeling victorious, the students were released. King, however, was not. In an odd twist, King was transferred to DeKalb County, Georgia, where he had once been arrested for driving without a license. Although he had paid the fine for that incident, the DeKalb officials insisted that King's arrest at Rich's was a violation of the terms of his suspended sentence. He was sentenced to four months hard labor.

The severity of the punishment brought the normally composed Coretta to tears. Martin, already stunned by the judge's pronouncement, was truly scared when he was transferred to Reidsville State Prison—in Klan country, hundreds of miles from Atlanta—in the middle of the night. He tolerated a cold cell, inedible food, and cockroaches, all for a minor traffic violation, until October 28, when he was suddenly let out. On the way home, Coretta told him why he had been released. The DeKalb judge had reversed his decision thanks to the intervention of a young senator from Massachusetts. His name was John F. Kennedy, and in 1960 he was the Democratic candidate for president of the United States. Kennedy was a well-spoken and charming politician who had a commitment to civil rights and sincerely believed segregation was wrong. But King felt that Kennedy, the son of a wealthy Boston family, did not understand the daily struggle of being a Negro in the United States. Still, Kennedy had come to his aid, and Martin was grateful.

Back in Atlanta, Martin was greeted by crowds singing the hymn "We Shall Overcome," which had become the theme of the civil rights movement. He stood in front of Ebenezer Baptist Church and thanked the senator who helped him, noting that he was a man of principle and courage. King never said he would vote for Kennedy, but Negroes who heard him speak assumed he would. Blacks who supported Richard Nixon, Kennedy's Republican opponent, changed loyalties. Daddy King was one of them.

The 1960 presidential election was one of history's closest. Those votes may have proved valuable. Kennedy won by a slim margin of 112,881 votes.

A third King child, Dexter Scott, was born in 1961, the same year Kennedy began his presidency. It was also the hundredth anniversary of Abraham Lincoln's inauguration. King had high hopes, both for the future of his baby boy and for Kennedy's ability to make civil rights an important issue for the country. King wrote that Kennedy should use his leadership to fight for a new, stronger civil rights bill, and put his power behind a "second Emancipation Proclamation," which would abolish segregation. He met with the president and his brother Robert Kennedy, the attorney general, about these matters but made little progress. Their energies were focused on an international crisis in Cuba. He would have to show them that civil rights mattered, even if it meant that he—and thousands of other Negroes—would go back to jail.

On October 25, 1960, King is led away from jail on his way to an appearance at traffic court. The four-month sentence he was given was eventually dropped.

5

Fighting Back

Despite progress at lunch counters, on city buses, and in schools, the country was far from integrated. Although the Supreme Court ruled that bus terminals with separate colored and white waiting and rest rooms were unlawful, most of these facilities remained segregated. On May 4, 1961, a group of blacks and whites set out to test this law. They belonged to an organization called the Congress of Racial Equality (CORE), and they called themselves Freedom Riders. The group boarded buses in Washington, D.C. Their destination was New Orleans. Their plan was to stop at bus stations in the South and try to use segregated areas. They hoped their nonviolent protest would make the nation pay attention to the problem of segregation.

What started out as an orderly demonstration became a nightmare. On May 14, Mother's Day, the first bus of Freedom Riders arrived at Anniston, Alabama. They were met by a mob of whites armed with knives, pipes, and bricks. The bus driver quickly pulled away, but outside the city the mob caught up with them. They tossed a bomb into the bus. Rushing from the flames and smoke, the riders fled from the burning vehicle only to be attacked. The second bus of riders

got through Anniston safely, but at Birmingham a group of local KKK members beat them with baseball bats, pipes, and

chains while the local police turned their backs. Many of the CORE activists were severely wounded in these attacks, and one—Walter Bergman—spent the rest of his life in a wheelchair as a result of his injuries.

Brave students in Nashville, Tennessee, wanted to keep the Freedom Ride alive. They drove to Alabama to board a bus but were turned away. They tried again, and finally, with

Freedom Riders sit on the ground after evacuating a bus set afire by a mob of angry whites outside Anniston, Alabama.

protection from the federal government, successfully boarded a Birmingham bus bound for Montgomery. Young Freedom Riders arrived at the city that witnessed the birth of the civil rights movement on May 20.

In Montgomery, all was strangely quiet as the riders filed off the bus. Suddenly a thousand angry whites wielding weapons descended on them. The mob brutally beat riders John Lewis, Jim Zwerg, and many others. The bloody scenes were aired on television and witnessed in person by presidential aide John Seigenthaler, who had been sent down to Alabama by Attorney General Robert Kennedy to assess the situation. In his efforts to save a woman from attack, Seigenthaler himself was hurt. Alabama Governor John Patterson supported the mob and vowed that if there were continued efforts to integrate his state, "Blood's going to flow in the streets." King could no longer be a quiet observer of these

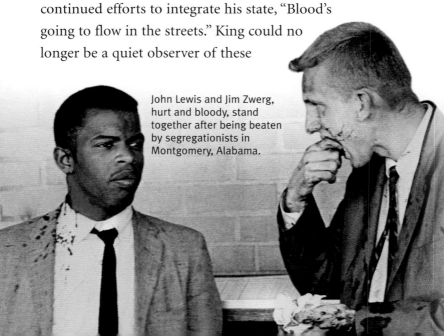

John Lewis and Jim Zwerg, hurt and bloody, stand together after being beaten by segregationists in Montgomery, Alabama.

events. The time had come for him to go to Montgomery.

On May 21, King arrived at Ralph Abernathy's church to address a mass meeting in support of the Freedom Riders. While King spoke inside, a mob of whites formed outside. Their shouts and jeers grew louder and louder. They began to throw rocks and tear gas through the church windows. King pleaded for calm as the congregation, trapped in the airless sanctuary, ducked flying glass. He then went to the church basement and phoned Attorney General Kennedy. Kennedy immediately sent in the National Guard to subdue the crowd. The people were able to leave the church unharmed.

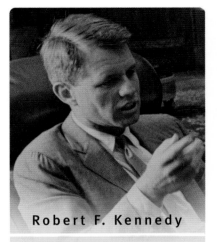

Robert F. Kennedy

Robert Kennedy was his brother's closest adviser. After JFK was killed, Robert won a seat as senator from New York and launched programs to help minorities and poor people. Youthful and passionate, he became a candidate for the presidency in 1968, but he was assassinated at age 42 on June 5, 1968, just after winning the California primary.

Robert Kennedy hoped that the Freedom Rides would end. He felt that the riders had proved their point. But CORE leader James Farmer disagreed. The rides would continue, right into the heart of the South—Jackson, Mississippi. During the summer of 1961, more than 300 riders rode into

King leads a long line of protesters on a peaceful march through Albany, Georgia, on December 16, 1961. The peace would not last.

Jackson, only to be arrested at their destination. With so many arrests and so much bad publicity, the future of the Jim Crow laws stood on shaky ground. In September, Robert Kennedy finally pressured the Interstate Commerce Commission (ICC) to issue regulations ending segregation at bus facilities. By November there were to be no more separate white and colored facilities. CORE won its battle. This victory inspired others to join the civil rights movement.

Trouble was also brewing in Albany, Georgia, where Negroes were struggling to desegregate bus terminals and register to vote, meeting resistance from the white community every step of the way. The Albany Movement, as the campaign was called, had been formed by a group of civil rights organizations, including the NAACP and SNCC.

When protesters marched down to the Trailways bus terminal in November to test the new ICC ruling, they were thrown into jail. Hundreds were held in miserable conditions, with dozens of people packed into cells that were supposed to hold only a few. There was no word about when they would be released. William G. Anderson, head of the Albany Movement, called King for help.

King flew to Albany with Ralph Abernathy. Met by crowds singing "Freedom" and "We Shall Overcome," King was moved to join their cause. The next day, he and Anderson went down to city hall to speak with the mayor. The mayor refused to see them. King and Anderson then led their followers— hundreds of men, women, and children—on a mass march through downtown Albany. At the bus station, they were stopped by the local police. Chief Laurie Pritchett came forward and warned the leaders that if they continued, they would be arrested. With calm dignity, King and the marchers knelt to pray. They were rounded up and taken off to jail.

Word soon came that the city was willing to negotiate with movement

Abernathy and King are arrested by Albany Chief of Police Laurie Pritchett (at right, with back turned) during a civil rights protest.

protesters. King and Abernathy were released on bail. But they had been misled. No progress had actually been made in talks with the city, and the situation for the rest of the prisoners was unchanged.

Chief Pritchett was a clever opponent. As protests continued in Albany, he never used violence to stop them. He understood that police brutality—like that used against the Freedom Riders—would earn public sympathy and support for King and his movement. He simply continued to arrest Negroes, and though King was imprisoned again for his activities in Albany, he could not get the city to react. One evening when a black woman brought food to demonstrators in jail, she was severely beaten. Negroes in Albany lost patience. That night,

James Meredith (right) is denied entrance to Ole Miss by Lieutenant Governor Paul Johnson (in glasses and hat.)

thousands of blacks retaliated. They attacked police with rocks and bottles. The movement was no longer nonviolent. King had lost the battle in Albany.

In the fall of 1962, the South would see more violence, this time at the University of Mississippi. In September, James Meredith, a veteran of the U.S. Air Force, tried to enroll as the first Negro student at "Ole Miss." Governor Ross Barnett vowed to protect the state's highly regarded educational institution from integration. He did not care about the Constitution or civil rights—and he would not back down. He denied Meredith access to the campus. President Kennedy was once again faced with a racial crisis. He ordered federal troops down to Mississippi to protect Meredith.

The scene on September 30, 1962, was frightening. Three hundred federal marshals circled the university's main building. Hundreds of Confederate-flag–waving whites gathered before them to await Meredith's arrival, not knowing that he had been brought to campus secretly the night before. The whites, armed with guns and knives, resented the presence of troops in their state. President Kennedy assured the public that the crisis at Ole Miss was under control, but that evening a marshal was attacked by a crowd member, releasing a full-scale assault on the troops. The marshals lobbed tear gas into the mob, which responded with gunfire. A French journalist covering the event for his newspaper was shot in the back, and another man died from a stray bullet. By morning, dozens of marshals had been shot and hundreds on both sides were wounded.

For the next few weeks, Oxford, Mississippi, looked like a battlefield. More than 20,000 troops were called up to keep peace. James Meredith won entrance to the university but spent his four years there painfully isolated from the other students. No one would speak to or sit with him. Martin felt this was not a true victory for integration. So much blood had been shed for one man. For King, there would be no celebration until all Negroes could attend the schools of their choice unchallenged. There was more work to be done.

Much of the day-to-day work of defeating Jim Crow was accomplished by Bob Moses of SNCC and David Dennis of CORE, who headed into small towns throughout the south encouraging people to register to vote. The simple act of voter registration often had dire consequences for blacks. Many who tried to do so lost their jobs—some lost their lives.

In 1962, government officials in Leflore County, Mississippi, penalized blacks who participated in the voter registration drive by cutting off the food surplus program that was critical to the

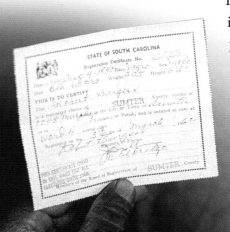

A black voter in South Carolina holds a new voter registration card—a result of CORE's work in small towns in the South.

survival of their families in winter. In order to strengthen their presence, several civil rights organizations, such as the NAACP, SNCC, and CORE, came together to form the Council of Federated Organizations, or COFO. COFO workers helped blacks fill out voter registration forms and seek government assistance, and they taught black children to read and write. COFO volunteers practiced nonviolence.

King recovered from the Albany Movement failure but admitted that he had tried to do too much there. He recognized that he should have focused on a particular cause, such as integrating lunch counters or buses, rather than on ending all segregation. Still, he was getting set for a new campaign when Bernice Albertine was born in March of 1963. He and Coretta called the baby "Bunny." Her arrival allowed Martin to spend some much-needed time with his family. Although Martin's travel schedule was hectic, he was a devoted father and never lost sight of the fact that he was working to better the future of his own children. Martin tried to protect his children from the pain of racial prejudice. But Yoki had already experienced the pain Martin had felt as a child when he could not attend movies or play in parks open only to whites. At age six, she saw a commercial on TV for an amusement park called Funtown. Yoki begged Martin and Coretta to take her there. But Funtown was closed to colored children. Sadly, they sat her down and told her about segregation.

6

Battling in Birmingham

Birmingham, located in the heart of Alabama, was known as the most segregated city in the South. There were two people working to keep it that way—Commissioner of Public Safety Eugene "Bull" Connor, who hated the very word "integration," and Governor George C. Wallace. At his inauguration as governor, Wallace delivered a forceful speech, declaring "Segregation now! Segregation tomorrow! Segregation forever!" The battle lines were drawn. King vowed to bring his nonviolent campaign to their doorstep. If SCLC could change Jim Crow laws in Alabama, the outlook was good for the rest of the South.

King and his staff moved into Birmingham, where local SCLC leader Fred Shuttlesworth had been preparing for mass demonstrations and boycotts of segregated facilities. The city had seen terrorist acts by whites against blacks—bombings, lynchings, and brutality—for years, but arrests were never made in these crimes. King knew that Bull Connor would not stand back, as Chief Pritchett had in Albany, and watch "niggers" take over his town. Despite the risks, King distributed, on April 3, 1963, a "Birmingham Manifesto," which demanded the desegregation of lunch counters, restrooms, and drinking fountains in downtown department stores. He warned that if steps were not made toward desegregation, boycotts and demonstrations would follow.

In nightly meetings at neighborhood churches he rallied local Negroes to join in the battle of Birmingham.

King called on these volunteers to form a "nonviolent army," trained in singing and marching, not rioting and killing. By April 10, Negroes were demonstrating in front of city hall and picketing local stores. Bull Connor met the orderly crowd with snarling police dogs. Protesters were hauled off to jail.

On April 11, King received an injunction from the State of Alabama prohibiting him, Abernathy, Shuttlesworth, and other SCLC organizers from conducting mass demonstrations in Birmingham. On Good Friday, the Christian holiday that commemorates the crucifixion of Jesus, King ascended the pulpit at Zion Hill Church and said the march would go on. He then led his volunteers downtown, until he came face-to-face with a shouting Bull Connor. Silently, King and Abernathy knelt before him in prayer. They were promptly arrested.

This was King's thirteenth arrest, but it was his first time in solitary confinement.

On April 12, 1963, arrested for staging protests in Birmingham, King is hauled into a police van by the seat of his pants.

Held alone in a narrow, airless cell without a mattress or pillow, he was in despair. Not only were conditions in the jail deplorable, but he knew that his organization had run out of bail money. He had no idea how long he and the other volunteers might be imprisoned. With so many supporters locked away in jail, the protests might lose momentum or stop altogether, and the battle of Birmingham would be lost. Easter Sunday was grueling for Martin, but on Monday he received good news. Harry Belafonte, a black entertainer who was committed to the movement, raised $50,000 for bail money. Also, King's jailers were suddenly kinder, bringing him a mattress and a pillow, and eventually letting him call Coretta.

Coretta was relieved to hear Martin's voice. She had not been able to get information about her husband after his arrest. In a panic, she phoned Robert Kennedy in Washington, who said he would help. Later, Coretta heard directly from President Kennedy, whose staff had called the Birmingham jail to check in on King. That explained the jailers' change in behavior. Still King remained in his cell, receiving visits only from his lawyers. On one of those visits they brought him a copy of a Birmingham newspaper. King was eager for any news about the campaign, but what caught his attention most was a statement signed by eight Alabama clergymen urging Negroes to abandon their protests and be patient in waiting for change. The writers were all white.

Entertainer and activist Harry Belafonte speaks to a large crowd at a civil rights rally in New York City in 1960.

King was not allowed to have paper and pencils in his cell, but he was determined to answer the clergymen's statement in an open letter that would explain the importance of the nonviolent civil rights movement. With a pen smuggled in by his lawyers and on scraps of newsprint and toilet paper, he composed his famous "Letter from a Birmingham Jail." In it he explained, "Freedom is never voluntarily given by the oppressor; it must be demanded by the oppressed," and reminded them that "We have waited for more than 340 years for our constitutional and God-given rights."

King was able to walk out of jail a few days later. Back on the streets of Birmingham, he found that the protests had weakened. The SCLC leaders needed more volunteers, but where could they find a new crop of

people willing to go to jail for the cause? They found their answer in Negro colleges, high schools, and elementary schools. Youngsters wanted a chance to join the movement. King was not sure it was wise to put children at risk. After all, there had been violence in Montgomery and Albany. In Bull Connor country, it could be worse. King thought it over and decided that black children who lived with Jim Crow faced the danger of lynchings and bombings every day. He would take a risk and let them march.

On Bull Connor's orders, Birmingham firemen aim their high-pressure hoses at a crowd of young protesters.

The Children's Crusade began on May 2, 1963. That day, more than 1,000 children, some as young as six, set out from the Sixteenth Street Baptist Church in orderly columns. Many were arrested. But on May 3, more excited youngsters showed up to participate—more than 2,500 of them. Carrying signs and chanting "We want freedom," they made their way downtown until they were stopped at barricades set up by Bull Connor and the local police and firefighters. Connor barked orders at the crowd, but the marchers refused to turn away. Then he bellowed, "Let 'em have it."

With news cameras recording the entire event, Connor's men unleashed snarling German shepherds. The dogs lunged at the

frightened children, who scattered wildly. Several people were badly bitten. At the same time, firemen aimed their powerful water hoses at the boys and girls, who were immobilized by the impact of the water. The force of the water pushed them against buildings and sent them sprawling to the pavement. TV viewers across the country watched in horror.

These scenes were repeated many times in the days that followed. On a prayer pilgrimage to the Birmingham jail on May 5, children knelt in front of Bull Connor's snapping dogs. This time, when Connor ordered the firemen to turn on the hoses, they would not respond. Even Connor's men were moved by the youngsters' bravery.

High school students peacefully protest in Birmingham, Alabama, during the Children's Crusade.

There were more than 3,000 people in jail and thousands more still protesting every day in the streets. By May 7, however, no progress had been made in talks with the city, and thousands of young marchers were again met by Bull Connor. This time Connor's forces used dogs, clubs, and cattle prods to disperse the crowd, and then herded the unsuspecting protesters into Kelly Ingram Park. There, cornered and confused, they were blasted by fire hoses. Movement leader Fred Shuttlesworth was knocked unconscious by a gust of water and had to be taken from the scene in an ambulance. The situation was out of hand.

Governor Wallace sent in hundreds of state troopers outfitted in riot gear to help Connor subdue the marchers. But after weeks of disorder in Birmingham, white business leaders had had enough. The city was a battleground, and the ugly war was being viewed on TV by millions of Americans. Reluctantly, Birmingham's business leaders agreed to work out a settlement with King. Within 60 days, lunch counters, fitting rooms, rest rooms, and drinking fountains in downtown department stores would, they promised, be integrated.

Relieved and exhausted, King returned to Atlanta, in time to spend Mother's Day with Coretta. But just hours later, he received a frantic call from his brother, A.D.

A protester falls while being forced by police into Kelly Ingram Park.

George C. Wallace

After losing his first bid for Alabama governor to a man who had support from the KKK, Wallace tried to appeal to voters on the race issue. He became a spokesman for segregation and served many terms in office. Over time, Wallace changed his position on race and was reelected as governor in 1982 with the support of many African-Americans.

A.D. King lived in Birmingham. His home had been bombed by whites—possibly Klan members. Segregationists had also destroyed much of the Gaston Hotel, which had been used as SCLC headquarters in Birmingham. A.D. reassured Martin that he was not hurt, but others had been injured, and now angry Negroes were taking to the streets, setting stores on fire and attacking policemen. Wallace's troopers were ready for them.

Full-scale riots were raging in Birmingham. King raced back to calm the city's black citizens and reassure white business leaders that he stood by their agreement. His presence had an almost magical effect. He would not allow the success of the Birmingham campaign to be spoiled by violence. The people listened.

The victory in Birmingham secured King's fame as the greatest spokesman for Negro people in the United States. For President Kennedy, the events in Birmingham were a sign that the country was truly ready for change—and new civil rights laws.

Daring to Dream

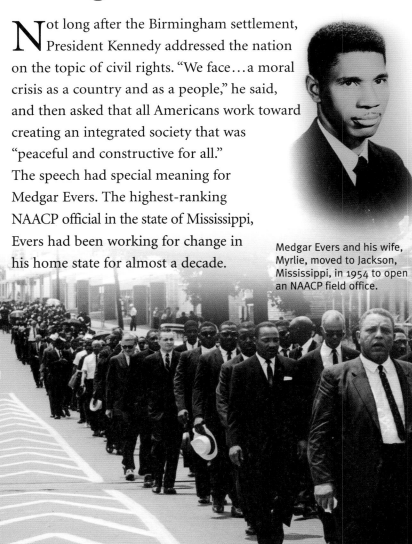

Not long after the Birmingham settlement, President Kennedy addressed the nation on the topic of civil rights. "We face...a moral crisis as a country and as a people," he said, and then asked that all Americans work toward creating an integrated society that was "peaceful and constructive for all." The speech had special meaning for Medgar Evers. The highest-ranking NAACP official in the state of Mississippi, Evers had been working for change in his home state for almost a decade.

Medgar Evers and his wife, Myrlie, moved to Jackson, Mississippi, in 1954 to open an NAACP field office.

As a young man, he had been blocked from registering to vote and denied entrance to law school because he was a Negro. Evers was a World War

II veteran. He returned from military service ready to fight for his country in a different way. He would fight for freedom.

A dedicated and courageous man, Evers had investigated lynchings in Mississippi, including the killing of Emmett Till. He had risked his life to help a black witness who testified against Till's white killers safely escape Mississippi, and he was an adviser to James Meredith, who challenged the admissions policies of Ole Miss. By 1963, he was living in Jackson, Mississippi, with his wife and children, where he was battling the city government over fair employment and integration. After listening to Kennedy's speech with other NAACP workers on June 11, 1963, Evers headed home to his wife, Myrlie, and their children. They heard his car door slam—and then they heard a shot. He was gunned down before he could reach the front door. His death provoked an outpouring of rage and grief far beyond Mississippi. Medgar Evers became a martyr of the civil rights movement. It was in memory of people like him that blacks made Washington, D.C., their destination in the summer of 1963. They traveled to attend the March on Washington for Jobs and Freedom,

Mourners at Evers's funeral, including Dr. King (second row, left), march in Jackson.

Dr. Martin Luther King, Jr., leads protesters through the streets of Washington, D.C., toward the Lincoln Memorial on the National Mall.

and to hear one of the most memorable speeches of their lives—delivered by Dr. Martin Luther King, Jr.

Washington, D.C., with its federal buildings and majestic monuments, was built on what was once a swamp. It is sweltering, humid, and bug-ridden all summer. On August 28, 1963, 250,000 people—black and white—decided that no such discomfort would keep them from marching in the nation's capital. From almost every state in the union, and by every means of transportation available, they arrived to join in the greatest gathering in the history of the civil rights movement. Carrying placards and singing spirituals, the crowd assembled before the statue of the man who wrote the Emancipation Proclamation. There were several speeches at the Lincoln Memorial that day, but only one is so familiar to America's schoolchildren that they can recite parts of it by heart. In the passionate voice that had inspired the faithful at the Ebenezer and Dexter Avenue churches, King said, "I say to you, my friends, so even though we face the difficulties of today and tomorrow, I still have a dream. It is a dream deeply rooted in the American dream. I have a dream that one day this nation will rise up and live out the true meaning of its creed: 'We hold these truths to be self-evident, that all men are created equal.'

"I have a dream that one day on the red hills of Georgia, the sons of former slaves and the sons of former slave owners will be able to sit down together at the table of brotherhood.

"I have a dream that one day even the state of Mississippi, a state sweltering with the heat of injustice, sweltering with the heat of oppression,

In the shadow of the Washington Monument, the Mall is packed with citizens who came to hear King and others speak at the March on Washington for Jobs and Freedom.

King opened his speech by saying the March on Washington would be the "greatest demonstration for freedom in the history of our nation."

will be transformed into an oasis of freedom and justice.

"I have a dream that my four little children will one day live in a nation where they will not be judged by the color of their skin but by the content of their character. I have a dream today!"

Overcome with emotion, King descended the podium into a sea of cheering well-wishers. For him, the speech had special meaning, because whites as well as blacks heard his message. As Abraham Lincoln had 100 years before, King reminded people of all races that they must work together to ensure a government that guarantees freedom for all.

After the march, the Kings attended a reception at the White House with President Kennedy and Vice President Lyndon Johnson. There was great optimism among them about the future of the movement and the civil rights bill. At that meeting Kennedy warned King about possible FBI surveillance of his activities, primarily by the agency's director, J. Edgar Hoover. Kennedy knew that many whites wanted to see King's movement fail. He cautioned King to be careful. King returned home to Atlanta to resume his duties at Ebenezer Baptist Church.

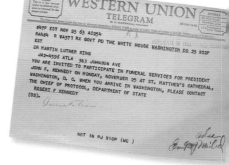

Robert F. Kennedy telegraphed King to invite him to the funeral of President Kennedy, a friend of the civil rights movement.

He was preaching there on Sunday, September 15, 1963, when a bomb went off in Birmingham.

The Sixteenth Street Church, which had served as a haven for marchers during the Birmingham campaign, was blasted by dynamite that morning. Four young girls, Addie Mae Collins, 14, Denise McNair, 11, Carole Robertson, 14, and Cynthia Wesley, 14, were in the basement preparing for their roles as ushers and choir members at a youth service. At 10:22 AM a blast shook the church. The girls were killed instantly. In all the violence that had been inflicted on blacks in their struggle for equality, nothing felt as vicious as this attack on innocent children. In grief and anger, the Negro community vented its rage by rioting in the streets of Birmingham.

Martin Luther King tried to comfort his people at a funeral service for three of the four girls. "God has a way of wringing good out of evil.... The innocent blood of these little girls may well serve as the redemptive force that will bring a new light to this dark city.... Indeed, this tragic event may cause the white South to come to terms with its conscience," he said. FBI investigators could not find the person or group responsible for the bombing.

Just two months later, on November 22, another tragedy upset the nation. President Kennedy was shot and killed on a trip to Dallas. Kennedy had grown to understand and support the civil rights movement, and now he was gone. As he had for Medgar Evers and the Birmingham children, King grieved for his friend and political ally and for a nation

King and Malcolm X, two men with differing ideas on civil rights, met for the first and only time on March 26, 1964, in Washington, D.C.

capable of so much violence.

Still, 1963 had been a glorious year for King. He was the first African-American selected as *Time* magazine's "Man of the Year," and his portrait was on the cover of the January 3, 1964, issue. He was as adored in America as Gandhi had been in India. But not all Negroes agreed with King's philosophy of nonviolence.

Malcolm X, a black leader of the Muslim faith, thought King was too accepting of whites. He believed that nonviolence was leaving Negroes defenseless against white domination and felt that black people should fight back—with violence if necessary—in their struggle to be free. Malcolm inspired a black nationalist movement. He did not work for integration, but wanted to keep the races separate. Malcolm's views weakened King's support among blacks in northern cities, who were impatient with the slow gains of nonviolent resistance. While King did not approve of Malcolm's teachings, he respected his intelligence. When Malcolm X was assassinated in 1965, King mourned his loss.

Throughout 1964, King and the SCLC worked furiously to integrate lunch counters in St. Augustine, Florida, and register voters in Mississippi in 1964. Just days after four

GHETTO

A ghetto is a section of a city in which minority groups live, usually because poverty, race, or class doesn't allow them to live elsewhere.

young civil rights workers were kidnapped and murdered in Mississippi, the SCLC's tireless efforts were rewarded. On July 2, 1964, Lyndon Johnson, who succeeded Kennedy as president, signed the Civil Rights Act of 1964. Johnson gave the pen he used to sign the bill into law to Reverend King. King said the Civil Rights Act was "written in the streets" by millions of brave Negroes. It not only addressed constitutional issues, such as school desegregation, but focused on economic ones, such as how to tackle poverty in black communities of the South as well as urban ghettos of the North.

At the end of 1964, King learned that he would receive that year's Nobel Peace Prize. Honored to be only the second African-American to earn the honor (Ralph Bunche, mediator of a truce between Arabs and Israelis, was the first), he vowed to give the $54,000 award to the civil rights movement. At his acceptance speech in Oslo, Norway, he asserted his continuing faith in humanity to break the bounds of racism and declared, "I still believe that we shall overcome."

President Johnson signs into law the Civil Rights Act of 1964.

chapter **8**

Marching in Selma

During the summer of 1964, a thousand college students, most of them white, went south to join a campaign called Freedom Summer, a major drive to register black voters. The young men and women also established Freedom Schools, which helped educate poor blacks and prepare them for the difficult literacy tests they had to pass in order to register to vote. The organizers of Freedom Summer hoped that the presence of white workers would bring attention to their cause. If white workers were beaten or jailed, the country would take greater notice than if the victims of such acts were black. However, no one could have

King points to Selma, Alabama—the heart of his voters' rights campaign—on a map during a meeting at an SCLC office in early 1965.

predicted the violence directed at the volunteers as they tried to help blacks claim their basic rights. Churches were burned and bombed, workers were clubbed and arrested.

That summer also brought together 80,000 blacks who joined the Mississippi Freedom Democratic Party in an effort to challenge the segregationist policies of their state's Democratic Party. Representatives of that group attended the national Democratic convention in Atlantic City to bring attention to the voting rights issue. On national television, party member Fannie Lou Hamer described the violence experienced by southern blacks who tried to vote.

King, too, focused on the problem of voting rights. Despite the passage of the Civil Rights Act, local police and politicians in the South still fought against ending Jim Crow.

In 1965, King decided to launch a campaign in Selma, where blacks had been turned away from the voting booth again and again. Out of 15,000 Negroes who were eligible to vote in Selma, only 350 had registered. Blacks outnumbered whites in that city, but they represented only one percent of the voters. King knew his presence would bring media attention to this injustice, and, as in Montgomery and Birmingham, he was ready to march.

Selma's black population was largely poor. Schools were still segregated despite the *Brown v. Board of Education* decision of ten years earlier. In 1965, the term "nigger" was heard on Selma streets more often than "Negro" or "colored." Selma's Sheriff Jim Clark was typical of many public officials

A young man brings attention to the cause of registering black people to vote. He was among the marchers heading from Selma to Montgomery.

there who eyed civil rights workers with suspicion and vowed that they would never allow Negroes to take over the state of Alabama. When young volunteers from SNCC came to town, a state judge blocked their efforts to rally blacks by banning Negroes' rights to hold group meetings. He also issued an injunction against marching. Sheriff Clark, ready with club and cattle prod, enforced the law. King decided to challenge Clark, just as he had defied Bull Connor. He and Ralph Abernathy arrived in Selma on January 2, driving over the Edmund Pettus Bridge toward the unpaved streets and rundown buildings of the "nigger" section of town.

At Brown Chapel that afternoon and in the weeks that followed, King and Abernathy rallied supporters with cries of "Give us the ballot!" By mid-January they were ready to confront Sheriff Clark. The first 50 people to march to Clark's office at the courthouse were arrested right away. Throughout the month, protesters who marched down to the courthouse were personally met by Clark, fully outfitted in a military uniform with a lapel pin that read NEVER.

Soon state troopers were called into Selma. With tensions rising, King gathered with 700 marchers at Brown Chapel on February 1 and announced that this was the day they would go to jail. He led the group down Selma's streets, and they were immediately arrested.

As the headlines reported that King was in jail, the Nobel prize-winner publicized the plight of Selma's Negroes by writing an ad that was published in *The New York Times*. He wrote, "Why are we in jail? Have you ever been required to answer 100 questions on government…merely to vote? Have you ever stood in line with over a hundred others and after waiting an entire day seen less than ten given the qualifying test? This is Selma, Alabama. There are more Negroes in jail with me than there are on the voting rolls."

King and Clark's forces clashed repeatedly, and the jails kept filling up. TV and newspaper reporters moved into Selma to cover events. Clark's deputies smashed protesters with billy clubs and herded them out of town with cattle prods. When blacks in nearby Marion organized a march of their own, state troopers were quick to apprehend the crowd at the town square. Panicked by the officers' swinging clubs, the people scattered. Jimmie Lee Jackson and his mother rushed to safety in Mack's Café. When Jimmie's grandfather walked in, bleeding from the blows he received from the troopers, Jimmie was desperate to get him to a hospital, but the troopers had blocked the exit and were clubbing the people trapped inside. As he lunged at an

The Edmund Pettus Bridge spans the Alabama River on the edge of Selma. The marchers met up with Clark's men here.

officer to protect his mother from being injured, the 25-year-old church deacon was hit in the stomach by a trooper's bullet. Though wounded, he managed to run from the troopers, but they chased him into the street, where he collapsed. He died days later.

Again, King found himself delivering a eulogy at a young person's funeral. His task was to help control the rage and bitterness people felt toward their white oppressors. Before a crowd of 2,000, King begged the weeping mourners not to retaliate with violence. James Bevel, an associate of King's, had a better idea. There would be a new march. This one would be longer—from Selma, Alabama, to the state capital in Montgomery. They would gather at the steps of the Alabama Capitol and directly petition Governor George Wallace to end police brutality. For 54 long miles, people would walk off their tension, and then they would make their voices heard.

King was preaching back in Atlanta at Ebenezer Baptist on March 7, but that Sunday his aide, Hosea Williams, and John Lewis of SNCC set out from Brown Chapel in Selma with more than 500 marchers. Carrying blankets, food, and water for their long trek, they headed down Highway 80 toward the Edmund Pettus Bridge. As they crossed the bridge, they stopped in their tracks. A column of state troopers, with riot gear and clubs, had created a wall through which they could not pass. An officer yelled through a bullhorn: "Turn around and go back to your church." He warned them that they had only two minutes to retreat.

Suddenly the state troopers lunged toward the passive crowd. Brandishing their clubs, they struck out at them. John Lewis's skull was fractured, and battered men and women lay on the ground like fallen leaves crushed underfoot. The troopers then released tear gas into the crowd, which sent the marchers staggering, choking, and gagging for air. In their agony, the protesters could hear the cheers of white spectators.

Sheriff Jim Clark (in glasses, holding billy club) stands with a deputy. It was on his orders that marchers were beaten on Bloody Sunday.

Jim Clark and his men had been waiting to make their entrance. They appeared on the scene with bullwhips and barbed wire, further beating back the crowd until, bleeding and hysterical, the protesters made their way back to Brown Chapel. More than 70 people were hospitalized. Afterwards, that day was known as Bloody Sunday.

Martin suffered tremendous guilt when he heard about the attack on his people at Edmund Pettus Bridge. He felt he should have been there to lead and comfort them. Desperate to find a way to help the black citizens of Selma, King sent telegrams to religious leaders across the country, pleading for support. The response was amazing. People across the nation had seen news clips of Clark's brutal attack on the marchers. Horrified, they too took action. Sympathy marches for the Selma protesters were held in cities across the country, and clergymen abandoned their parishes to head for Alabama. Their spirits lifted, the Negroes of Selma vowed to march again.

On March 9, Martin had a problem. A judge issued a restraining order officially banning another march. But 1,500 protesters were ready and willing to cross the Edmund Pettus Bridge toward Montgomery. King explained to worried government officials who feared more violence that blacks had been patient for 300 years and could wait no more.

That afternoon, he led his followers down Highway 80. At the bridge a U.S. marshal called out: "This march will not continue." King asked him if they could pray. Silently, the ministers and marchers knelt and bowed their heads. Before the impenetrable column of armed and helmeted men, one of the ministers asked God to clear their path. Miraculously, the troopers stood aside.

However, King did not take his followers over the bridge that day. He would not disobey a court order and decided to fight for legal permission to conduct the march. He asked many of the clergymen who had some to Selma if they could stay. James Reeb, a white Unitarian minister from Boston, was one who agreed to do so. After witnessing the events of Bloody Sunday, he was committed to the cause.

Civil rights activist John Lewis (in light-colored coat at bottom left) is attacked by a state trooper with a billy club. His head injury required hospital treatment.

Reeb ate out with two other white ministers that night. They went to a Negro restaurant. While walking back to SCLC headquarters after dinner, the group turned down the street of a rough all-white hangout, the Silver Moon Café. Out of the shadows came four white men. "Hey, you niggers!" someone called. In a flash, the men came at the ministers with clubs. Reeb was smacked in the head. He lapsed into a coma and died two days later.

Because Reeb was white, his death had an even greater impact on public opinion than that of Jimmie Lee Jackson. This new violence so moved President Johnson that he promised to draft a stricter voting rights bill and submit it to Congress. On March 15, Johnson went on television and made an appeal on behalf of

Martin and Coretta lead the nine-day march from Selma to Montgomery, a distance of 54 miles.

King stops to change his socks on the way to Montgomery.

the bill. Days later the judge lifted the court injunction that blocked the Montgomery march.

On March 25, an exuberant King and a very weary group of marchers arrived in Montgomery. Across the street from the Dexter Avenue Church, where King had preached years before, they stood at the state capitol singing "We Shall Overcome." Governor Wallace refused to come out and receive their petition, but he must have heard their message.

Civil rights worker Viola Liuzzo was shuttling tired marchers between Selma and Montgomery in her Oldsmobile that evening when a car full of Klansmen raced up alongside her. One of them fired a .38 caliber pistol through her window, killing the white mother of five instantly.

Another martyr to the movement, she did not live to see President Johnson sign the Voting Rights Act into law on August 6, 1965. The new law banned literacy tests and unreasonable restrictions. Blacks would now be free to vote people like Jim Clark and George Wallace out of office.

LITERACY
Literacy is being able to read and write.

Expanding the Crusade

By 1965, Martin Luther King's leadership of a nonviolent civil rights movement was seen as a huge success. Since the Montgomery bus boycott of 1955, most of the outward signs of Jim Crow in the South had disappeared. There were no longer WHITE and COLORED sections on buses, and lunch counters served people of all races. Many black children went to school with white children, and most black voters were not turned away at the polls. With new civil rights laws in place, the federal government took a greater role in supervising integration in the South,

Looters take goods from a liquor store at the corner of Santa Barbara and Avalon Streets in Los Angeles, California, during the August 1965 riots.

and in enforcing the laws in states that weren't cooperating.

Still, the new laws did not necessarily improve the day-to-day living conditions of black citizens. King had focused all his efforts on the plight of Southern blacks. But in the North, particularly in the cities—such as Chicago, Philadelphia, and New York— many blacks lived in terrible poverty. Crime plagued the residents of city ghettos. Schools were in turmoil, with run-down buildings, not enough staff, and out-of-date textbooks. Many students dropped out before graduating from high school. They had little hope for the future. Jobs were scarce for the undereducated, particularly if those people were black.

King was aware that there was de facto segregation in the North, even though Jim Crow laws did not exist there. He visited the slums of New York City and marched with followers in Roxbury, Massachusetts. Asked by Chicago's black leaders to help them win "quality integrated education" for black students, King felt it was his duty to take the crusade up to the Land of Lincoln. As he was preparing to launch his Chicago campaign, King came under attack from militant black groups that had run out of patience with the slow pace of the nonviolent movement. Young blacks who could hardly

afford the bus fare across town saw that even poor white families had more comfortable houses and cleaner streets than they did. They could not contain their anger. The worst violence occurred in the poor, overcrowded Watts section of Los Angeles on August 11, 1965, where riots broke out, with residents looting and burning everything in their path. Thirty-four people were killed, 900 were injured, and $46 million in property was destroyed. King tried to explain to the mayor of Los

Martin and Coretta look out from the top middle window of their apartment building in Chicago, Illinois.

Angeles that Watts exploded because Negroes living there had no jobs, the police treated them like common criminals, and the city didn't seem to care.

Martin strongly believed that people committed to the civil rights movement needed to live with those whose cause they were fighting for. "You can't really get close to the poor without living and being here with them," he said to reporters. Coretta helped him move into an apartment at 1550 South Hamlin Avenue in Chicago in January 1966. Located in a Negro area called North Lawndale, it was dingy

and poorly heated. He was paying $90 a month in rent for a two-bedroom apartment—more than white families often paid for five bedrooms. His fellow slum dwellers were delighted to have him in the neighborhood. Never before had they received any attention—not from the press or the city. Chicago's Mayor Richard Daley was not thrilled to welcome this new resident. King had been quick to criticize the city government for not doing enough to help Chicago's ghettos, which were plagued by rats, inadequate schools, and crime-ridden streets. King knew he had to inspire Chicago's black community to stand up for itself, but he recognized that asking the people to commit to nonviolence was going to be a challenge. He spent long days organizing in Chicago's Negro churches and equally long nights speaking with young gang members about putting down their weapons.

King soon found that he had two strong opponents in Chicago—Mayor Daley and black people themselves. Daley had his own campaign to combat poverty in Chicago and argued that it was working just fine. He worked hard to make political alliances with Negroes in the city to lure them away from King. King felt that Daley's programs weren't working, but he found it difficult to convince Negro voters, who had more confidence in their long-time mayor than in a newcomer from the South—even if the newcomer was a Nobel Prize winner.

With his efforts in Chicago losing steam, King and the SCLC staff came up against a problem that was even more

A pin announces the March Against Fear, which was held in honor of the injured James Meredith.

threatening. The nation was turning its attention to the war in Vietnam. With U.S. soldiers at risk on foreign soil and antiwar demonstrations being held at home, the civil rights movement was no longer the priority of President Johnson and congressional leaders. How could King get it back on track?

King was in Atlanta trying to find the answer when he learned that James Meredith, the man who had integrated Ole Miss as the first black student, had been shot. Meredith was wounded by an attacker while conducting a one-man March Against Fear, a march for voting rights that began in Memphis, Tennessee, and was to end in Jackson, Mississippi. He was recovering in a Memphis hospital. King rushed down to see him and was joined there by Floyd McKissick, the national director of CORE, and Stokely Carmichael, the new chairman of SNCC. The three black leaders held very different views about the future of the civil rights movement. After the violence in Selma, Carmichael found that he could not watch Negroes being beaten by whites without fighting back. McKissick, too, took a more militant approach. He thought blacks needed to band together against whites to earn political and economic power. King, of course, felt they were both wrong. But they decided to put aside their differences and, with Meredith's blessing, they set out on Highway 51 to continue the protest

he had started. It was on that trek that King came face to face with Black Power.

Along the highway, people were drawn to King. People rushed up to shake his hand, while others who couldn't get close to him were satisfied just to get a passing glimpse of the leader who meant so much to them. The marchers from SNCC and CORE, however, were not as impressed by him as their members had been in the early days of the civil rights movement. Under Carmichael and McKissick's influence, they became restless. Some questioned the purpose of a nonviolent march. Others

Black Panther Party

Founded in 1966 by Huey P. Newton and Bobby Seale, the Black Panther Party believed that violent revolution was necessary to achieve civil rights. The party called on black people to arm themselves in the struggle for freedom. However, the Black Panthers were not just a militant group; they demanded reforms in housing, education, and employment, too.

refused to sing "We Shall Overcome," saying that its message was too passive for the times. A few carried guns. When white bystanders in Mississippi harassed the group, Carmichael and his followers chanted hateful slogans back at them. The cries of "Freedom!" heard in Montgomery,

DISSENTERS

Dissenters express opinions that differ from those accepted by other people.

Birmingham, and Selma were being drowned out by a new slogan—"Black power!"

Carmichael told his followers that it was time to stop taking abuse from whites. He said, "The only way we gonna stop them white men from whuppin' us is to take over. We been saying freedom for six years and we ain't got nothin'." King begged Carmichael to see that black supremacy was just as racist as white supremacy—and that violence was not the answer. Martin spent 1967 trying to heal the wounds of the movement.

At the same time, he joined another crusade—the American peace movement. The Vietnam conflict, which grew into a full-scale war by the late 1960s, drew a lot of criticism. Many Americans felt this war was unnecessary. In siding with South Vietnam against North Vietnam, we were, they felt, defending one unjust government against another. Lives were being lost daily in a war we could not win. One of the most prominent and outspoken dissenters was preacher, civil rights activist, and Nobel Peace Prize winner Martin Luther King, Jr.

Martin was horrified by images he saw on TV of Vietnamese children left dead or orphaned by the bloodshed in their country. Our own soldiers were burning their villages and blowing up their fields. And King was outraged that the United States was spending billions of dollars in a foreign land rather than on the

streets of Chicago, Selma, or Memphis, where blacks continued to be plagued by crime and poverty. Wasn't it odd, he reflected, "We were taking the black young men who had been crippled by our society and sending them eight thousand miles away to guarantee liberties in Southeast Asia which they had not found in southwest Georgia and East Harlem. So we have been repeatedly faced with the cruel irony of watching Negro and white boys on TV screens as they kill and die together for a nation that has been unable to seat them together in the same schools."

King's antiwar comments provoked harsh criticism. Several newspapers faulted him for trying to take over the peace movement;

Villagers from Darlac Province in Vietnam flee as U.S. Special Forces troops evacuate a battle site. TV news coverage of the war fueled antiwar feelings.

they said he should stick to civil rights. His own supporters questioned the wisdom of tackling world peace when the movement needed his undivided attention. The worst blow came from Lyndon Johnson. Determined to have a military victory in Vietnam, the president seethed at King's words. Soon the FBI—in particular its director, J. Edgar Hoover— was keeping an even closer eye on King's activities.

The campaign in Chicago had taught Martin that new tactics were necessary to keep the civil rights movement alive in America. The sit-ins and marches that were so successful in the South could not stop the widespread violence that was erupting in the North. In June of 1967, King published a book called *Where Do We Go from Here: Chaos or Community?* In that book, Martin asked an important question: "Other immigrant groups such as the Irish, the Jews, and the Italians

Thurgood Marshall in conference with President Lyndon Johnson, who appointed him to the Supreme Court

started out [in America] with similar handicaps [to Negroes], and yet they made it. Why haven't Negroes done the same?"

The answer, thought King, was that none of those other groups had come to America as slaves. None had been made to feel inferior solely because of the color of their skin. Still, one could learn from other immigrants. Italians, Jews, and Irish had not separated from one another. They had worked together, forming trade unions and political alliances. The Black Power movement, with its call to break away from white society, was, in King's eyes, taking the wrong direction. He begged blacks to put aside the shame of their sad history and recognize their strengths. "We must say to ourselves and the world," he declared, "'I am somebody. I am a person. I am a man with dignity and honor.'" Tell your children that "black people are very beautiful."

One could look with pride at the strides blacks had made in the late 1950s and early 1960s. Just as King's book hit the bookstores, a former NAACP lawyer, Thurgood Marshall, was named to the Supreme Court. He was the first African-American to serve as a Supreme Court justice. There was hope, but also hard work ahead. With the rise of violence in poor black communities and the reluctance of whites to help solve it, King felt that drastic measures were needed to unite the races. He imagined a mass civil disobedience campaign in Washington, D.C., which would bring thousands of unemployed Negroes and supporters of all backgrounds to the capital. Blacks could no longer confine their protests to a single city—they had to address the nation.

chapter 10

Striking in Memphis

Martin called his new project the Poor People's Campaign. He began to mobilize groups from all over the United States to join in demonstrations for better jobs and higher pay. Knowing that lawmakers were distracted by the Vietnam War, he vowed to continue the protest as long as necessary to

Striking workers walk past armed National Guardsmen on Beale Street in Memphis, Tennessee.

refocus the government's
attention on the needs of the
American people. In private he
worried: Would SCLC be able to
control the crowds that would come to march in Washington?
Could they raise the money to bring people to Washington?
Would the rallies anger President Johnson and FBI director
J. Edgar Hoover? Would they retaliate against him and the
movement? Was it worth the risk?

<aside>
STRIKE

A strike is a protest that calls a halt to activities until certain demands are met.
</aside>

With these questions unanswered in the winter of 1968,
King took a break from the campaign and flew down to
Memphis, Tennessee. There, black sanitation workers were
on strike. They asked the city for better working conditions.
They also wanted higher wages. White workers were being
paid more, and the strikers wanted equal pay. The city's
answer was "No." The strikers vowed to stay off the
job until their demands were met. Skirmishes
with police followed, and tensions in the black
community were rising. Each day the striking
workers lined the streets of Memphis wearing
bold signs that read I AM A MAN, meaning,
"I am a human being and I deserve respect."
They marched to city hall. The city refused to
negotiate and got a court order to stop the
marches. Black leaders in Memphis knew they
needed help. That was when they called King.
Martin checked into the Lorraine Motel near the

King is surrounded by leaders of the sanitation strike shortly after his arrival in Memphis on March 28, 1968.

Memphis waterfront on March 18 to prepare for a mass meeting at Mason Temple.

That evening, the Atlanta preacher practically lit the room on fire. When his extraordinary voice rose, the audience rose with it. He reassured his followers that the strike was worthwhile: "We can all get more together than we can apart. And this is the way we gain power. Power is the ability to affect change, and we need power. And I want you to stick it out so you will be able to make Mayor Loeb and others say 'Yes,' even when they want to say 'No.'" The room exploded with singing and clapping. A big march was planned for March 22.

On March 21, a man with an unusual accent phoned a local Memphis radio station and warned that King would be shot if he marched in Memphis. That same day a blizzard

surprised the city of Memphis, so the demonstration was rescheduled for March 28. The delay gave King a chance to fly to New York for meetings about the Poor People's Campaign. He left no organizers in Memphis. He felt that Memphis was safe and that his nonviolent campaign would work. On Tuesday, March 28, he and Ralph Abernathy returned to Memphis and headed to Clayborn Temple where 6,000 restless people were ready to march.

Something did not seem right. With King and Abernathy leading in front, the crowd seemed to beat down on them rather than walking calmly behind. King was waving to well-wishers when he flinched at the sound of broken glass. Black teenagers began to smash store windows. That's when he noticed the BLACK POWER signs—and a unit of Memphis police fully outfitted in riot gear. King, horrified at leading a violent demonstration, yelled at his organizers to call off the march. While the marchers struggled to get back to their churches and their homes, King's friend James Lawson stopped a car and hustled King and Abernathy inside. They were whisked away from the scene and driven to the Holiday Inn Rivermont, where they watched the sad outcome of the event on TV.

Downtown the police had sprayed mace at the looters— and then opened fire. Hundreds of stores were ruined, dozens of people were injured, and one 16-year-old black boy was gunned down. Martin was heartsick. It was supposed to have been a nonviolent march. Who were the black looters? How come he had not known about them? Would this threaten the success of his grand campaign in Washington? Martin couldn't stop thinking about the boy who had been killed—and he couldn't sleep.

By the next morning, however, Martin had a new plan. He could not abandon Memphis until he proved to the city—and the country—that nonviolent resistance was still possible and

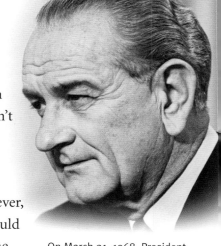

On March 31, 1968, President Lyndon Johnson told the American public in a TV announcement that he was not a candidate for reelection.

would work. He told the press that he accepted responsibility for the events of the day before. He had not known about the youth groups who planned the violence. He should have. He would know better next time, and he would march again—in April.

Despite his confident statement to reporters, King spent a difficult few days back in Atlanta. He was depressed about reports in newspapers across the country. As he had feared, many people now doubted that he could run a successful nonviolent campaign in Washington, and they linked his name with rioting.

Martin's staff members sensed deep sadness in him that they had not seen before. Ralph Abernathy, still King's closest

friend, and advisers Jesse Jackson, Walter Fauntroy, and James Bevel tried to boost his spirits, while SCLC workers Andrew Young and Bayard Rustin recruited the clergy and civil leaders in Memphis to work at the next march. They also held workshops on nonviolence.

In the midst of all this preparation, an announcement from President Johnson shocked many U.S. citizens, including King. Johnson was facing a difficult race against Eugene McCarthy for the Democratic nomination in the coming election. McCarthy was a popular candidate among antiwar activists, who were fed up with Johnson's persistent bombing of Vietnam. In a televised statement, Johnson announced he was reducing the scale of the conflict in Vietnam. He realized that the war had divided the country and that America needed to unite. Then he solemnly added, "I shall not seek, and I will not accept, the nomination of my party for another term as your president." A critic of Johnson's policy in Vietnam, King was relieved by this news. Without Johnson, he might be able to put civil rights back in the forefront

The Lorraine Motel was one of the few motels in Memphis that would accept black guests.

of the nation's mind and move forward with the Poor People's Campaign.

On April 3, one day before King was shot, Hosea Williams, Jesse Jackson, King, and Ralph Abernathy stand on the balcony of the Lorraine Motel. King is in about the same position he would be when the shot that killed him was fired.

A bomb threat on King's plane delayed his return to Memphis, but he successfully checked into room 306 at the Lorraine Motel on April 3. He had arrived in good spirits but grew worried again about the march as evening approached. There was a rally for supporters planned at Mason Temple that evening. Martin was in no mood to attend. However, when Abernathy begged him to address the 2,000 followers who had already gathered there, Martin gave in.

It was a rainy night, but, dry and warm inside, people were elated to hear the man who had forced Americans to come to terms with racism and segregation. King said he was happy God had brought him to Memphis. He urged the black community to show support for the striking sanitation workers. The question, he said, is not "If I stop to help the sanitation workers, what will happen to my job?" but "If I do not stop to help the sanitation workers, what will happen to them?" This "dangerous unselfishness" is what won civil rights victories in Montgomery, Birmingham, and Selma. They could have it in Memphis, too, he insisted. The audience erupted in cheers.

King seemed to revisit his whole life at that pulpit at Mason Temple. He talked about being stabbed at the New York book signing, about his operation and recovery, and about the little girl who wrote saying she was glad he had not sneezed. And he said he, too, was glad that he hadn't sneezed, because if he'd died, he would have missed the sit-ins and freedom rides, the civil rights bill, and Selma. He mentioned the bomb threat that had delayed his flight that morning and the threats that accompanied him into the streets of Memphis, and he admitted:

> Well, I don't know what will happen now. We've got some difficult days ahead. But it really doesn't matter with me now. Because I've been to the mountaintop. And I don't mind. Like anybody, I would like to live a long life. Longevity has its place.

CONVICT

A convict is a person serving a prison sentence, or who has served one in the past.

But I'm not concerned about that now. I just want to do God's will. And He's allowed me to go up to the mountain. And I've looked over. And I've seen the promised land. I may not get there with you. But I want you to know tonight, that we, as a people, will get to the promised land. And so I'm happy tonight. I'm not worried about anything. I'm not fearing any man. Mine eyes have seen the glory of the coming of the Lord.

It was his last speech. That night an escaped convict named James Earl Ray arrived in Memphis. From his hotel room, Ray could see the Lorraine Motel and the balcony of room 306. He had not come to support the sanitation workers.

On April 4, 1968, King met with his staff to discuss the upcoming march. They needed to make sure that the protest was nonviolent. In the motel conference room, they discussed their concerns with leaders of a militant student group. The SCLC organizers hoped to convince the group to join the nonviolent movement and then carry the message of nonviolence into the schools. King had lunch at the motel with Ralph Abernathy and enjoyed a visit from his brother, A.D. Later that afternoon King's aides informed him that the local court, which had been concerned about more violence, had given permission for the march. There would be no legal hurdles, no court injunction. King's spirits soared.

The SCLC staff was in a celebratory and playful mood as they got ready to go out to dinner. A local clergyman, Reverend Samuel Kyles, had invited them to his home for real southern soul cooking—pigs' feet, blackeyed peas, and greens, Martin's favorite foods. Kyles and King were on the motel balcony watching King's young aides joke around in the parking lot below. James Bevel and James Orange were roughhousing, and King teased Bevel, the smaller man, "Don't let him hurt you." He then urged Jesse Jackson to come to dinner and reminded him to put on nice clothes: "No blue jeans, all right?"

It was time to go, and Kyles led the way down to the parking lot. King lingered a moment. In that instant a single bullet from a high-powered rifle hit his face. He was knocked over by the force. King was lying on the balcony floor holding his throat, a pool of blood spreading around him. His aides below were yelling, "Take cover!" Ralph Abernathy came rushing out to the balcony. Trying frantically to stop the bleeding, he urged his friend not to be afraid.

By the time the ambulance arrived, King's pulse was faint. At the hospital doctors worked frantically to help him. While King's aides clasped hands in prayer outside the emergency room, Martin Luther King, Jr., died. Ralph Abernathy could have been speaking to the entire black community when he turned to the young men and said, "Now Martin is gone from us. Now we are alone."

chapter 11

Mourning a Leader

Coretta King learned of the shooting from a friend and headed to the airport. On the way there, she learned that Martin had died. She had endured segregation, the bombing of her home, and constant threats on her husband's life. Now she would endure his death and take on a new role as his widow. Feeling that her place was with her children, she returned home to tell them the news.

At Ebenezer Church, Martin's parents were weeping. They had learned of their son's death on the radio. The child who asked too many questions, who hurt for the poor as they waited on breadlines, whose voice had the power to move entire congregations, was now a martyr to the movement he had led.

April 5, 1968: two young men walk on a glass-littered street in front of a burning building during the rioting in Washington, D.C., that followed King's assassination.

The nation hurt, too. Not since John F. Kennedy's assassination had there been such shock. *The New York Times* called King's shooting a "national disaster" for blacks and whites alike. Around the globe, world leaders expressed their horror both at the tragic event of King's killing

and at the racism that plagued American democracy. There was anger, too. King, who had despised

Coretta Scott King walks with her children and the Rev. Abernathy in Memphis in honor of her husband.

violence, was gunned down. Stokely Carmichael raged that "when white America killed Dr. King, she declared war on us." He told his followers, "Get your gun."

As if in answer to his command, American blacks vented their anger in violence. Riots erupted in more than 100 cities. Dozens of blacks were killed, and tens of thousands of National Guards were called in to put out the fires and patrol the streets. Washington, D.C., looked like a battleground, with cars burning and whole buildings demolished. A white man was dragged from his car and killed. Troops were stationed on the street corners.

Coretta King knew that her husband had unfinished business in Memphis. She and Ralph Abernathy decided to march in Memphis to show the city—and the world—that

King's nonviolent campaign and his spirit were very much alive. On April 8, Coretta and her three oldest children walked with Abernathy and 19,000 supporters in a memorial march. Eight days later, the city settled the sanitation strike.

While King's body was being flown home to Atlanta for the funeral, a massive manhunt was under way for his killer. A rifle had been found, but its owner had escaped.

Martin's casket is put on an airplane for the trip home to Atlanta.

There was still no arrest by April 9, the day of King's funeral. Ralph Abernathy conducted the service at Ebenezer Church that day, where hundreds of mourners packed the sanctuary and tens of thousands waited outside in the heat to hear the eulogy over loudspeakers. Daddy King dissolved in grief by the casket of his older son, while Coretta, shielded by a black veil, led her children to say a final good-bye to their beloved father, whose cause had so often kept him from home.

Black celebrities arrived to pay their respects—Harry Belafonte,

Coretta Scott King, in a black veil, arrives at the funeral of her husband, Martin Luther King, Jr.

Mahalia Jackson, Lena Horne, Dick Gregory, and Sammy Davis, Jr. Dignitaries, too, descended on the city. Robert Kennedy and his wife, Ethel, arrived; Vice President Hubert Humphrey represented President Lyndon Johnson; and Jacqueline Kennedy, widow of President John F. Kennedy, came to share the community's sorrow. King's aides and adversaries came, too—James Bevel, Andrew Young, Walter Fauntroy, Jesse Jackson, John Lewis, Floyd McKissick, and even the militant Stokely Carmichael. Abernathy's service was followed by the playing of Martin's favorite hymns. Then, the silent congregation listened to a tape of Dr. King, in which he proclaimed, "But I just wanted to leave a committed life behind. Then my living will not be in vain."

Martin's casket was loaded onto a mule cart, symbolizing the Poor People's Campaign that King would now never lead. Accompanying the wagon were King's supporters— more than 50,000 of them—many dressed in farmer's overalls.

Mourners file past King's coffin to pay their last respects. More than 60,000 people stood outside the church listening to the funeral service over loudspeakers.

They made their way to Morehouse College, where King had been inspired to become a preacher. There, King's mentor, Benjamin Mays, thanked God for the life of Martin Luther King, Jr., who was able to see beyond hate and work for peace and justice. His body was then taken to South View Cemetery, where he was buried near Grandmother Williams.

James Earl Ray was one of the FBI's 10 Most Wanted Fugitives following the shooting. After he was imprisoned, Ray suggested he was part of a larger plot to kill King.

Martin had loved the language of Negro slave spirituals. Many of these songs of freedom had been sung in Montgomery, Selma, and Birmingham as protesters were carted off to jail. Others were heard on the Freedom Rides and at mass meetings in churches throughout the segregated south. Now, the lyrics to his favorite were etched on his tomb.

> Free at last, free at last
> Thank God Almighty
> I'm free at last.

There were several people absent from King's funeral, most noticeably President Johnson. Perhaps he never forgave King for his opposition to the war in Vietnam. Still, on April 11, 1968,

just two days after King was laid to rest, Johnson signed the Civil Rights Act of 1968, which prohibited discrimination in the sale or rental of housing.

The rifle used in King's shooting was linked to James Earl Ray, a white high-school dropout and petty criminal, who had escaped the morning of April 4 from a prison in Missouri. It was discovered that the murder weapon had been fired from the bathroom window of a boardinghouse that faced the Lorraine Motel. Witnesses said they saw a man run from that house with a bundle. But the trail stopped there.

On June 8, 1968, authorities caught up with the suspect, who had fled to Europe after King's murder. According to witnesses at Heathrow Airport in London, where Ray was arrested, the alleged killer put his head in his hands and wept. Initially Ray admitted buying a rifle like the one used to kill King and confessed to renting a room in the boardinghouse. In March of 1969, he was sentenced to 99 years in prison for the assassination of Dr. Martin Luther King, Jr. But after awhile, Ray changed his story. He mentioned handing the weapon to a man named "Raoul," and he suggested that the murder was the work of a conspiracy. Until his death in 1998, he would not identify

Raoul or any other members of the so-called plot to assassinate King. Any chance of discovering the truth in the case died with him.

Ralph Abernathy, King's loyal friend and his second-in-command in the movement, now had the uncomfortable task of filling the shoes of America's civil rights leader. He knew that those shoes could never fit him. King had an intellect, style, and presence that could not be matched. Ralph spent the grief-filled weeks after King's death flying from city to city to rally support. It was his burden in the summer of 1968 to organize the SCLC's Poor People's Campaign. What had already been an uphill battle for Martin was an enormous struggle for Abernathy, who

The Mule Train, symbol of the Poor People's Campaign, crosses the Potomac River into Washington, D.C. The campaign went on without King.

insisted to reporters that he had not asked for his new role as civil rights leader; it had been thrust on him by King's death. He declared that a "sick America" took the life of his friend, and though he tried to show strength at marches and meetings, he seemed sick at heart, too.

A button announcing the Poor People's Campaign

By the summer, tents had been built on the National Mall in Washington, D.C., and the site was named Resurrection City by the 2,000 protesters who settled there. Fifty thousand people, black and white, marched behind Abernathy on Solidarity Day, June 19, but the Poor People's Campaign did not live up to King's vision. Martin was the glue that had held the movement together. The tents were torn down two months later, after the committee's land use permit expired. Slowly the SCLC began to unravel.

Tragedy soon struck King's family again. Eighteen months after the assassination, A.D. King, who took Martin's place next to Daddy King at Ebenezer Church, was found drowned in his swimming pool. Five years after that King's mother, Alberta, was shot to death by a black youth while playing the organ at Ebenezer's Sunday morning service.

Daddy King told the congregation at Martin's funeral that "It was the *hate* in this land that took my son away from me." The influential patriarch who never stopped missing his son left the pastorate after his wife's death, but he did not shy

away from the public eye. As he had during Martin's life, he continued to attend civil rights rallies and meetings, and spoke at the Democratic National Conventions in 1976 and 1980. In 1984, after attending services at Ebenezer, Daddy King died of a heart attack.

It seemed to be Coretta Scott King who became most visible after Martin's death. Of course, she had always been one of his greatest supporters. Martin Luther King, Jr., once confessed to an interviewer that he could not take credit for leading Coretta to the path of nonviolence—it was a path they took together. From the outset of their relationship, she was as concerned with racial and economic injustice and peace as he was. After Martin's death, she devoted herself to spreading Martin's philosophy around the globe. Weeks after she marched in Memphis and buried her husband, she attended an anti-Vietnam rally in New York and then worked with Ralph Abernathy on the Poor People's Campaign in Washington.

In 1969, Coretta published a memoir, *My Life with Martin Luther King, Jr.*, and worked on plans for the Martin Luther King, Jr. Center for Nonviolent Social Change in Atlanta, which was established as a memorial to Dr. King's life and philosophy. The King Center's mission is to develop programs that educate people about Dr. King's life, work, and belief in nonviolent change. Coretta, like Jacqueline Kennedy, became a symbol of a nation's greatest grief and its greatest hope. Her presence at protests and political events

served as a reminder of what the movement was all about. Throughout the 1970s and 1980s she worked for world peace, traveling to South Africa to protest apartheid, an unjust system of racial segregation that ended in the 1990s.

King's children, who suffered the loss of their father when they were so young, grew to be active in preserving the ideals for which he worked. But decades after King's murder, his family remained unsettled by Ray's imprisonment. They thought there may have been a conspiracy, as Ray himself suggested. There were theories that J. Edgar Hoover and the FBI may have had a hand in the tragic scene at the Lorraine Motel. Dexter Scott King met with James Earl Ray in 1997, and asked him, "For the record: Did you kill my father?" Ray replied, "I didn't, no, no." Dexter looked at the accused man and said, "My family and I believe you." However, no further evidence has turned up to support Ray's claim.

Coretta Scott King addresses the 1988 Democratic National Convention in Atlanta, Georgia.

chapter **12**

Honoring the Man, Not the Myth

Christine King Farris, Martin's older sister, wants people to know that her brother "was no saint, but an ordinary man." Yolanda King, Martin's older daughter, has remarked that it is easy to romanticize events when looking back. King's former friends and aides have cautioned that if we turn King into a hero we forget that he was human. He becomes a myth rather than a martyr. They want people to remember that Martin Luther King, Jr., became swept up by changes in this country and, because of his charisma and

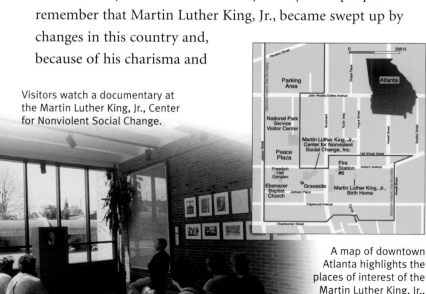

Visitors watch a documentary at the Martin Luther King, Jr., Center for Nonviolent Social Change.

A map of downtown Atlanta highlights the places of interest of the Martin Luther King, Jr., National Historic Site.

character, rose to lead. He did not create the civil rights movement, but became one of its most accomplished, outspoken, and passionate members. And they want people to understand that ordinary citizens can bring about extraordinary events, as proved by the participants of the Montgomery bus boycott, the Children's Crusade in Birmingham, the lunch counter sit-ins, and the Freedom Rides.

King's compassion for his fellow man and inspiring speeches assured him an attentive audience, and when he told his congregation or his followers, "You are somebody," they listened. One of the beliefs he communicated so well—to the people who worked with him and to all Americans—was that every man has dignity. Blacks who had been treated as second-class citizens since the time of slavery needed to hear this and believe it. King convinced them that they had the power to act.

The civil rights movement did not die with Martin Luther King, Jr., but it certainly changed. It was already taking a new direction when Martin was killed. Jim Crow laws were King's original target. It was relatively easy to get people to fight for a seat on the bus or a place at the lunch counter. The injustice of that kind of segregation was felt daily and was visible for all to see. His later goals—ending poverty, improving housing, stopping violence—were much bigger and more difficult to achieve. Before his death, King confessed that there would be tough days ahead. Despite his

Congressman John Lewis of Georgia addresses the 2000 Democratic National Convention in Los Angeles, California.

doubts about the future, he was committed to working for the good of humanity. King hoped to achieve the dream he spoke about in Washington in 1963. After his death, many of his followers continued to work toward that dream.

One of those people was SNCC leader John Lewis. Lewis, who had heard King preach as a young man and became his devoted follower, was elected congressman from Georgia in November 1986. After his election, he moved into an office in Washington, D.C., not far from where Dr. King delivered his famous "I Have a Dream" speech. Lewis was one of the speakers that day in 1963. He remained a strong supporter of nonviolence. Reflecting back on those decades, Lewis feels that the beatings and arrests he endured as an activist in the 1960s were worth suffering because they gave him the courage to stand up for his rights. "Sometimes when you want to change things or make a statement or

Andrew Young and Jesse Jackson both entered politics in the years following King's assassination.

send a message," says Lewis, "you have to simply get in the way." Now in his ninth term in office, Lewis represents Georgia's Fifth District, which includes the city of Atlanta as well as parts of surrounding counties.

Julian Bond became chairman of the board of the NAACP in 1998.

Another man who worked to preserve Dr. King's work was Jesse Jackson. Jackson was with Martin at the Lorraine Motel when King was shot. A member of SCLC since 1965, and leader of its Operation Breadbasket project in Chicago, Jackson left that organization in 1971 to found his own group, People United to Save Humanity (PUSH). Like his mentor Martin Luther King, he became a highly visible civil rights leader and used his magnetic personality to instill a sense of pride in young African-Americans. Twice in the 1980s, Jackson attempted to earn the Democratic presidential nomination, but was unsuccessful. Still, his campaigns convinced Americans that a black man could run for—and one day win—the presidency of the United States. Since 1986, Jackson has headed the Rainbow Coalition, an organization of minority groups working for social change.

Reverend Ralph Abernathy found that replacing Martin Luther King, Jr., as civil rights leader was a monumental task.

Andrew Young was a pastor in the South when he became caught up in America's civil rights movement. Young joined the SCLC to work on the voter registration drives and was an aide to King until King's murder. He then worked for Ralph Abernathy at SCLC until 1970. Young entered politics and served several terms as a U.S. Congressman. In the House of Representatives, he supported funds for social programs and blocked funding for the war in Vietnam. He later served as the U.S. ambassador to the United Nations during the Carter presidency. Andrew Young was mayor of King's hometown, Atlanta, Georgia, from 1981 through 1989.

As a Morehouse College student, Julian Bond participated in sit-ins at Atlanta's segregated restaurants. Like John Lewis, he was a founder of SNCC and served as its communications director from 1961 to 1965. Bond was elected to the Georgia assembly, serving four terms as state representative until 1974. He then served as state senator until 1987. Bond remembers that when he learned of King's death, he felt like he had lost a member of his own family. King inspired him to enter public life and made him feel that he could make a difference. In 1998 Julian Bond was elected chairman of the board of the NAACP.

Ralph Abernathy died in 1990, 22 years after his best friend, Martin Luther King, Jr. Martin began to take the death threats more seriously in the last months of his life. He asked Ralph to be his successor, and Ralph did not let him down. From the days of the Montgomery bus

boycott, Abernathy had been not only a friend to the movement leader, but an organizer in his own right. He stayed with SCLC until 1977. Although Abernathy was often criticized for not being as strong a leader as King, he served as an important personal link to the King years. He became pastor of a Baptist church in Atlanta after leaving public life and wrote his recollections of the nonviolent protests from Montgomery to Memphis in an autobiography called *And the Walls Came Tumbling Down*. Like the nation, Abernathy never truly recovered from that gunshot on the Lorraine Motel balcony.

In addition to carrying on the ideals of the movement, Martin's followers wanted to remember his life, promote

The Civil Rights Memorial, designed by Maya Lin, sits outside the Southern Poverty Law Center in Montgomery, Alabama. The table in the foreground is carved with a timeline of events of the civil rights movement. Water spills over both the back wall and the table, encouraging visitors to touch the memorial.

...UNTIL JUSTICE ROLLS DOWN LIKE WATERS AND RIGHTEOUSNESS LIKE A MIGHTY STREAM

MARTIN LUTHER KING JR

his philosophy of nonviolence, and preserve his legacy. They asked the government to pass a bill making Martin Luther King, Jr.'s birthday—January 15—a national holiday. Like the movement itself, the battle for the King holiday was waged by many people over many years.

It began four days after the shooting in Memphis, when a Democratic congressman from Michigan, John Conyers, introduced legislation for the birthday observance. Coretta Scott King launched her own lobbying efforts for the holiday, as did SCLC, which submitted signed petitions with millions of signatures to House delegates. But eleven years after Martin's death, the bill died in Congress.

As her husband proved over and over again, it takes time to bring about change. Coretta, as president of the King Center, resumed a campaign in the early 1980s to gain official recognition for Martin Luther King Day. She wrote to politicians and civic leaders throughout the country, and they united to lobby for the holiday. The coalition established an office in Washington, D.C., where they could keep up the pressure on lawmakers. Finally, the holiday bill, sponsored by Senator Ted Kennedy, the younger brother of President John F. Kennedy and Robert Kennedy, was signed into law by President Ronald Reagan on November 3, 1983. The first official Martin Luther King Day was celebrated in January 1986.

Martin might have been surprised at the extraordinary bill effort, but he would surely have been pleased to become

Students spend Martin Luther King Day painting a mural commemorating Dr. King and the civil rights movement.

one of the only social leaders in the world to have a holiday named for him. Another such leader was Mahatma Gandhi, whose birthday is a national holiday in India.

For schoolchildren, Martin Luther King's birthday has become an occasion to learn about civil rights and tolerance. Many teachers have their students read or listen to Martin's "I Have a Dream" speech, which is a deeply moving experience. King's family hopes that people will use the holiday for spiritual reflection and to sponsor activities that bring diverse communities together.

Many people wonder, What would have happened if Dr. King had lived? Would he have been able to keep up the hectic pace of fighting the battle for civil rights? Would followers of Malcolm X and the Black Panthers have lured future generations away from King's nonviolent message? Would he have been able to bring national attention to the poverty that plagued the nation's ghettoes?

What seems certain is that King's deep commitment to

DIVERSE

Diverse communities are ones that include people of different races, classes, and religions.

119

nonviolence would not have wavered despite his doubts about the future.

I am concerned about a better world. I'm concerned about justice. I'm concerned about brotherhood. I'm concerned about truth. And when one is concerned about these, he can never advocate violence. For through violence you may murder a murderer but you can't murder murder. Through violence you may murder a liar, but you can't establish truth. Through violence you may murder a hater, but you can't murder hate. Darkness cannot put out darkness. Only light can do that.

Moments after he delivers his "I Have a Dream" speech, Dr. Martin Luther King, Jr., waves to the crowd in response to thunderous applause.

Martin Luther King's beliefs allowed him to exclaim "We Shall Overcome" as police herded

EMPOWERED

When you are empowered, someone or something gives you the right or authority to act.

Birmingham children into jail cells, to sing "Ain't Gonna Let Nobody Turn Me Around" as he marched toward armed troopers in Selma, and to foresee a day when he could shout "Free at Last" with his followers in Memphis. His sense of right and wrong gave him the courage to fight for the greatest civil rights gains in the twentieth century. He dared black Americans to hope and act. With his words and deeds, he opened the door to a once-forbidden world and empowered his people to walk through.

> I must confess, my friends, the road ahead will not always be smooth. There will still be rocky places of frustration and meandering points of bewilderment. There will be inevitable setbacks here and there. There will be those moments when the buoyancy of hope will be transformed into the fatigue of despair. Our dreams will sometimes be shattered and our ethereal hopes blasted.…Difficult and painful as it is, we must walk on in the days ahead with an audacious faith in the future.

Events in the Life of Martin Luther King, J

December 5, 1955
After Rosa Parks refuses to give up her seat on a Montgomery city bus, King is appointed president of MIA at a mass meeting at Holt Baptist Church, Montgomery.

January 15, 1929
Martin Luther King, Jr., is born in Atlanta, Georgia.

June 18, 1953
Martin and Coretta Scott marry in Alabama.

February 25, 1948
Martin is ordained and becomes the assistant pastor at Ebenezer Baptist Church, Atlanta.

September 20, 1958
King is stabbed by a deranged woman in New York City at a book signing for *Stride Toward Freedom*.

1929

September 20, 1944
Martin begins his freshman year at Morehouse College.

May 6–8, 1951
Martin Graduates from Crozer Seminary School.

February 2–March 10, 1959
Martin and Coretta travel to India.

September 1, 1954
Martin begins working as pastor at Dexter Avenue Baptist Church, Montgomery, Alabama.

January 10–11, 1957
King is named chairman of the newly formed Southern Negro Leaders Conference, later known as the Southern Christian Leadership Conference (SCLC).

August 28, 1963
At the March on Washington for Jobs and Freedom, King delivers his legendary "I Have a Dream" speech to a crowd of 200,000 demonstrators.

April 4, 1967
In a speech at Riverside Church in New York, King demands that the U.S. end the war in Vietnam.

April 9, 1968
King is buried in Atlanta, Georgia.

April 3, 1968
King delivers his final speech, "I've Been to the Mountaintop."

November 3, 1983
President Ronald Reagan signs the bill making the third Monday of every January the Martin Luther King, Jr., national holiday. The first M.L.K. Day is celebrated in 1986.

December 10, 1964
King receives the Nobel Peace Prize in Oslo, Norway.

1983

April 16, 1963
During conflict in Birmingham, Martin writes his famous "Letter from a Birmingham Jail" in prison.

January 26, 1966
King moves to Chicago to bring attention to the plight of the poor in that city.

March 28, 1968
King marches with striking sanitation workers in Memphis, Tennessee. The protest ends in violence.

April 4, 1968
Martin Luther King, Jr., is shot and killed at the Lorraine Motel, Memphis.

Bibliography

Branch, Taylor. *Parting the Waters: America in the King Years, 1954–1963.* New York: Simon & Schuster, 1988.

Bullard, Sara. *Free at Last: A History of the Civil Rights Movement and Those Who Died in the Struggle.* New York: Oxford University Press, 1993.

Carson, Clayborne, ed. *The Autobiography of Martin Luther King, Jr.* New York: Warner Books, 1998.

Darby, Jean. *Martin Luther King, Jr.* Minneapolis: Lerner Communications Company, 1990.

Eubanks, W. Ralph. *Ever Is a Long Time: A Journey into Mississippi's Dark Past.* New York: Basic Books, 2003.

Farris, Christine King. *My Brother Martin: A Sister Remembers Growing Up with the Rev. Dr. Martin Luther King, Jr.* New York: Simon & Schuster Books for Young Readers, 2003. Illustrated by Chris Soentpiet.

Frady, Marshall. *Martin Luther King, Jr.* New York: Viking Penguin, 2002.

Garrow, David J. *Bearing the Cross: Martin Luther King, Jr., and the Southern Christian Leadership Conference.* New York: William Morrow and Company, 1986.

Hakim, Rita. *Martin Luther King, Jr. and the March toward Freedom.* Connecticut: The Millbrook Press, 1991.

Haskins, Jim. *Power to the People: The Rise and Fall of the Black Panther Party.* New York: Simon & Schuster Books for Young Readers, 1997.

King, Casey, and Osborne, Linda Barrett. *Oh, Freedom! Kids Talk about the Civil Rights Movement with the People Who Made It Happen.* New York: Alfred A. Knopf, Inc., 1997.

King, Coretta Scott. *My Life with Martin Luther King, Jr.* New York: Henry Holt, 1969, rev. 1993.

King, Martin Luther Sr. (with Clayton Riley). *Daddy King: An Autobiography.* New York: William Morrow and Company, 1980.

Oates, Stephen. *Let the Trumpet Sound: A Life of Martin Luther King, Jr.* New York: HarperCollins, 1982.

Smith, Vern E., and Meacham, Jon. "King's Legacy." In *The Civil Rights Movement,* edited by Nick Treanor. Michigan: Greenhaven Press, 2003, pp. 120–125.

Turck, Mary C. *The Civil Rights Movement for Kids: A History with 21 Activities.* Chicago: Chicago Review Press, 2000.

Washington, James M. *I Have a Dream: Writings and Speeches That Changed the World, Martin Luther King, Jr.* San Francisco: HarperCollins, 1992.

Works Cited

Page 6: "I'm going to turn this world upside down." *My Brother Martin,* p. 26

Page 11: "He discovered that his Victorian-style house…" *Let the Trumpet Sound,* p.11

Page 12: "That's a *boy* there…" *Let the Trumpet Sound,* p. 12

Page 15: "That night will never leave…" *The Autobiography of Martin Luther King, Jr.,* p.10

Page 17: "On our way here we saw some things…" *The Autobiography of Martin Luther King, Jr.,* p. 11

Page 21: "character, intelligence, personality, and beauty" *Parting the Waters,* p. 95

Page 25: "Emmett Till, a native of Chicago…" *Free at Last,* pp. 44-45

Page 27: "We have took this type of thing too long…" *Let the Trumpet Sound,* p. 65

Page 28: "Martin, Martin, come quickly!" *Let the Trumpet Sound,* p. 67

Page 29: "If we are wrong, the Supreme Court of the nation is wrong." *Let the Trumpet Sound,* p.71

Page 33: "A victory for justice and democracy" *Let the Trumpet Sound,* pp. 103-104

Page 35: "Give us the ballot…" *The Autobiography of Martin Luther King, Jr.,* p. 108

Page 39: "Are you Martin Luther King?" *The Autobiography of Martin Luther King, Jr.,* p. 117

Page 39: "Dear Dr. King: I am a ninth grade student…" *The Autobiography of Martin Luther King, Jr.,* p. 118

Page 41: "We don't serve colored here." *Free at Last,* p. 22

Page 48: "blood's going to flow in the streets" *Let the Trumpet Sound,* p. 175

Page 56: "Segregation now! Segregation tomorrow! Segregation forever!" *Let the Trumpet Sound,* p. 213

Page 59: "Letter from a Birmingham Jail" *I Have a Dream,* p. 83

Page 60: "Let 'em have it." *Let the Trumpet Sound,* p. 234

Page 64: "We face…a moral crisis as a country…" *Free at Last,* p. 61

Page 67: "So, I say to you my friends…" *I Have a Dream,* p. 104

Page 69: "God has a way of wringing good out of evil…." *The Autobiography of Martin Luther King, Jr.,* p. 231

Page 75: "Why are we in jail?" *Let the Trumpet Sound,* p. 342

Page 77: "Turn around and go back to your church." *Let the Trumpet Sound*, p. 347

Page 79: "This march will not continue." *Let the Trumpet Sound*, p. 351

Page 80: "Hey, you niggers!" *Free at Last*, p. 78

Page 84: "You can't really get close to the poor without living and being here with them" *Let the Trumpet Sound*, p. 388

Page 88: "The only way we gonna stop them white men from whuppin' us…" *Let the Trumpet Sound*, p. 400

Page 89: "We were taking the young men who had been crippled by our society…" *The Autobiography of Martin Luther King, Jr.*, p. 338

Page 91: "I am somebody. I am a person…" *Let the Trumpet Sound*, p. 424

Page 94: "We can get more together than we can apart." *The Autobiography of Martin Luther King, Jr.*, p. 353

Page 97: "I shall not seek, and I will not accept…" *Let the Trumpet Sound*, p. 482

Page 99: "I've been to the mountaintop." *I Have a Dream*, p. 201

Page 101: "No blue jeans, all right?" *Let the Trumpet Sound*, p. 490

Page 101: "Now Martin is gone from us." *Let the Trumpet Sound*, p. 492

Page 103: When white America killed Dr. King, she declared war on us." *Let the Trumpet Sound*, p. 494

Page 111: "Did you kill my father?" "Making the Calendar" by Paul Andrews in *Seattle Times* online (http://seattletimes.nwsource.com/mlk/holiday/mlkday.html). Abridged version of article that appeared on January 15, 1985.

Page 112: "no saint, but an ordinary man" *Bearing the Cross*, Epilogue, p. 625

Page 114: "Sometimes when you want to change things…" John Lewis interview with Philip Brookman in *Corcoran Gallery of Art, A Capital Collection.* London: Third Millennium Publishing, 2002, p. 220

Page 120-121: "…I am concerned about a better world." *I Have a Dream*, p. 178

Author's Note

I am grateful to Joanna Banks at the Anacostia Museum and Center for African American History and Culture, Smithsonian Institution, for her helpful comments and suggestions. Special thanks to Peter, Nicholas, and Oliver Pastan, my best readers, and to Elizabeth Brimage, for sharing with me memories of her childhood in the segregated South.

DK Publishing, Inc., would like to thank: MacAllister Publishing Services, LLC; Laaren Brown and Lenny Hort; and Skip Mason, College Archivist at Morehouse College

For Further Study

The **King Center** (www.thekingcenter.com) in Atlanta, where visitors can learn about Martin Luther King, Jr.'s life and his message of nonviolence. Not far from the Center is King's birthplace on Auburn Avenue and the **Ebenezer Baptist Church**, both now museums run by the National Park Service. If you can't get to Atlanta, take a virtual tour at www.npg.gov/malu

The **National Civil Rights Museum** (www.civilrightsmuseum.org) opened in Memphis in 1991 at the site of the Lorraine Motel, where King was assassinated. It chronicles the history of America's civil rights movement through collections, exhibits, and educational programs.

Alabama (www.800alabama.com) has opened to the public many historic sites of the civil rights movement, including the **Rosa Parks Museum**, the **Civil Rights Memorial**, and **Dexter Avenue Church** in Montgomery; the **Sixteenth Street Baptist Church** in Birmingham; and the **Edmund Pettus Bridge** in Selma.

Watch *Eyes on the Prize* (Boston: Blackside, Inc., 1987–1990. PBS Home Video), an outstanding documentary series about the civil rights movement. See live footage of many of the marches, speeches, and historic events described in this book.

Browse through the **Martin Luther King, Jr. Papers Project** at Stanford University (www.stanford.edu/group/king/) and access the interactive timeline, with photos, audio recordings, and video clips of King and the civil rights movement.

Index

Picture Credits